Focusing

Eugene T. Gendlin, Ph.D.

D0036745

A Bernard Geis Associates Book

Bantam Books

I very much appreciate Max Gunther's
invaluable editorial help with this book.

FOCUSING
A Bantam Book

PUBLISHING HISTORY
Everest House edition published December 1978
A Selection of MacMillan Book Clubs (Behavioral Science) April 1979
Excerpted in *Lifestyle*, November 1980
Bantam revised edition / May 1981
Bantam mass market reissue / August 2007

Published by
Bantam Dell
A Division of Random House, Inc.
New York, New York

Bantam Books and the rooster colophon are
registered trademarks of Random House, Inc.

ISBN 978-0-553-27833-0

Printed in the United States of America
Published simultaneously in Canada

www.bantamdell.com

OPM   51   50   49   48   47   46   45   44   43   42

"I continue to use the focusing technique. We have found it a most valuable tool."

—O. Carl Simonton, M.D.,
Simonton Cancer Center

"Learning to access and dissolve personal problems by focusing on the language and wisdom of the body was a historic discovery. Gendlin's genius has stood the test of time."

—Harville Hendrix, Ph.D., author of
Getting the Love You Want

"An original, innovative, exciting book."

—Carl Rogers, Ph.D.

"*Focusing* is a beautiful and meditative approach to psychotherapy and personal growth. It offers a deep parallel to the practice of mindfulness in a carefully developed and sensitive way."

—Jack Kornfield, author of *A Path With Heart*

Contents

Focusing Now:

An Introduction to the 25th Anniversary Edition

Twenty-five years ago, when focusing was new, I shocked a colleague at the University of Chicago by saying "The unconscious is the body." By now an emphasis on the body as a source of information and innovation is not new. But exactly how one can tap into this source is not yet widely known. Only from the Focusing Community can one get well-developed and -tested instructions for direct access to embodied knowledge and the new steps that come from it.

Today people live at various distances from this bodily source. I tell therapists: When your clients say something important, put your hand between your own stomach and chest, and ask them: "If you attend here, what comes in your body about this?" Therapy will immediately deepen with those clients who are already close to this source. The other half will ask: "What do you mean?"

Check yourself. Notice where in my next few sentences you no longer know what I'm talking about. We can take you on further from there.

You have a bodily orienting sense. You know who you are and how you come to be in this room, reading this page. To know this you don't need to think. The knowing is physically sensed in your body and can easily be found. But this bodily knowing can extend much more deeply. You can learn how to let a deeper bodily felt sense come in relation to any specific situation. Your body "knows" the whole of each of your situations—vastly more aspects of it than you can think. Here you find an intricate bodily knowledge and new steps that want to come, and will come if you can wait here.

After you find this deeper level, it takes practice to stay here. In a difficult moment, most people cannot hold on to the body-sense of the situation long enough for steps to come. Focusing can train you to do this. Most people don't know how to let the unclear felt sense "open" into a whole field of intricate detail from which new steps of thought and action emerge.

Focusing is now a worldwide network. People who know focusing ask: "What would be a right next step here?" But this can seem insane to the rest of our society. How could new realistic ideas and action steps arise from the body? Isn't the body just a machine? How can more come from the body than evolution, language, and culture have built into it?

In philosophy, the "objectivists" hold that human experience is an illusion emanating from brain structures and chemistry. Their opponents, the "relativists," hold that human experience is just a product of one of the many cultures, histories, and languages. Underneath the variety there is nothing at all.

My philosophy leads to new concepts in physics and biology, to understand the human body differently. Your body is not a machine, but rather a wonderfully intricate interaction with everything around you, which is why it "knows" so much just in being. The animals live intricately with each other without culture and language. The different cultures don't create us. They only add elaboration.

The living body is always going beyond what evolution, culture, and language have already built. The body is always sketching and probing a few steps further. Your ongoing living makes new evolution and history happen—now.

You can sense your living body directly under your thoughts and memories and under your familiar feelings. Focusing happens at a deeper level than your feelings. Under them you can discover a physically sensed "murky zone" which you can enter and open. This is the source from which new steps emerge. Once found, it is a palpable presence underneath.

Social policy still assumes that human beings and animals are nothing but what science presents. For example, genetic engineering is now creating a cow-pig. It will have all lean meat. The company will corner the market for agricultural animals, never mind that the cow-pig is in pain. How we treat each other is often similar. Humans disappear in the current kind of science. Our science cannot even study the scientists themselves, and how they create the scientific concepts.

Science is not a game. Its truth is based on empirical testing. You wouldn't want to get on an untested airplane. We need our wonderful machines to work. But the basic method of this science renders everything it studies machines.

This kind of science need not be the only kind. The holistic science of ecology shows that more than one kind of science is possible. My philosophy adds another kind, a first-person science that can study itself! It centers on the body sensed from inside, where new things arise. Using focusing, we have developed "Thinking At the

Edge" (TAE), teachable steps to articulate something new in the field in which you work.

Our research on focusing is a small example of this potentially great new science. A long series of studies from tape-recordings and tests show that therapy has better outcomes when clients focus. Many other effects of focusing have also been measured—for example, better functioning of the immune system. Focusing has been applied in many contexts, including schools, businesses, spiritual groups, and creative writing.

When people first discover the power of focusing, they may think it is all they need. But focusing adds a deeper bodily level to other methods and can improve them. It cuts across the others and should be combined with anything else that can develop us as persons.

More than 600 certified focusing trainers around the world are available on your private telephone for one or several hours. You can also find a "Focusing Partner" on our Web site with whom to divide time and take turns, usually also on the phone. Focusing Partnerships are not friendships, not therapy, not family. Focusing Partnerships are a new social institution. Let me explain the need for it.

Currently the cultural routines and roles that used to connect us are insufficient. We have to innovate all day, find new ways to be a woman, man, wife, husband, parent, teacher, executive, old person, young person. Our close relationships tend to fall apart. "Nobody seems to fit with me," people say. Each person is intricate inside, and lonely. Modern urban society is atomized.

For a while it seemed that just expressing our feelings would help our close relationships—just blurt everything out. But what the other person hears can be so very different from what you meant to say, and sometimes hurtful. Similarly, we often react in ways that shut the other person down.

Therapists can listen to clients much more easily than to their own friends and loved ones. With people who are close, one's whole life rises or sinks with each little bit one hears. But one can peacefully accompany clients to deeper levels where the steps of change and healing come. Then the clients can relate much more deeply and freely to their own close friends and family. The new pattern of Focusing Partnerships makes this advantage of therapy available to everyone. A Focusing Partner costs nothing. You take turns. This new institution is changing the atomization of society.

During my time I am silent for some stretches and I speak some of the time. I say nothing I don't want to say. Speaking from far inside lets me hear myself and live connectedly in a receptive interaction.

Partners give no advice, judgments, or comments. They may repeat something back just to check: "I think you are saying..." But they need only say when they cannot follow, so that I can rephrase what I said. But my partner will pay close attention, wanting to grasp every wrinkle of what I mean.

A regular Focusing Partnership improves one's life immensely. I would not want to do without mine. In fact, I have two. I use my time for focusing or for whatever I wish. When my turn begins I feel how inviting it is—it is just for me. I might know what I want, or spend some minutes, scanning. I think: "I might talk of this...or perhaps that . . . well, perhaps first focus quietly. . . . I could have any of those things."

The Focusing Institute provides a few hours of telephone training in focusing, listening, and the experience of being listened to in a focusing way. Then you can select a partner from our Partnership Pool on the Web (www.focusing.org).

With focusing, one knows that the human being in front of us is more than any method, any set of beliefs, purpose, or project. We limit whatever we do for the sake of what is always more important: keeping people unobtrusive company with whatever they are up against. To give people just our simple presence lets them be and breathe. We listen for what they mean to convey, and add nothing else. It makes for maximal closeness with minimal imposition.

—Eugene T. Gendlin, 2003

Focusing:

A Tool for Changing Times

Focusing, the technique described in the pages of this book, is uniquely suited to our turbulent times when so many old forms are crumbling and old roles are vanishing. Most of us are having to invent, discover, and create the next steps of our lives without a light, a map, or a relevant tradition. We are trying to keep apace of rapidly changing technology, trying to understand ourselves and our relationships, seeking ways to be well, looking for meaning in our work and a new center of gravity within ourselves.

In a classic series of essays, the anthropologist Anthony C. W. Wallace described the phenomenon of cultural "awakenings." Such movements are triggered by stress, he observed. The "mazeways" of the culture, the customary sequences of behavior, are blocked. People cannot move into the roles they anticipated; their lives do not unfold in the ways they had been led to expect.

Under the duress of disintegrating social forms, a few creative individuals—Wallace called them New Lights—propose a way out: new pathways through the cultural maze. At first there is a "nativist" backlash, in which traditionalists urge a reversion to the old ways, but eventually, out of historic necessity, the New Lights prevail. Their ideas are adopted, and the society moves into a new era.

Clearly our culture is in the early stages of the transition Wallace described. Every aspect of our society, every institution, is challenged. The political structure, the medical and educational establishments, the economy, the family, religion, the workplace—all are undergoing change. We have no collective maps.

"Many people today are struggling with a baffling fact," Eugene Gendlin writes. "The old patterns that are supposed to make life work—and once did—no longer serve. Being a parent today, for example, doesn't work if we try to do it as our parents did, yet no other form is established for us to follow. We have to make it up as we go along...."

The old patterns were once useful, he acknowledges. Except for a few nonconformists, most people historically fitted themselves to their roles. "Only a small number of educated and thinking people *created* roles and patterns."

But today a large mass of people are educated and literate, with expanded needs to be creative. They feel confined by stock roles and emotions. They have feelings "far more complex than accepted roles either demand or offer."

Because of the radical changes we are undergoing as a culture, we have new, "unclear" feelings, emotions and sensations for which there is no common pattern. We are trying to create new forms appropriate to a new time. And we have an exciting, unprecedented opportunity. "If we accept ourselves and each other as form-makers, we will no longer need to force forms on ourselves or each other."

Eugene Gendlin and his co-explorers of the focusing

process are New Lights in this awakening, offering not only cultural alternatives but a tool for understanding our unclear feelings and inventing new patterns for living. Focusing is a key to personal momentum and unfolding, a dynamic process that can guide us through the tricky mazeways of a new world.

Like any powerful, new idea, focusing is not readily described in old terms. It moves us into unfamiliar territory, the realm of creative potential that we have usually considered the province of artists and inventors.

Our brains and bodies know far more than is normally available to us. We are conscious of only a fragment of what we deeply know. The central nervous system perceives and processes a great body of information that is stored outside the range of everyday awareness. Some of this information is best handled on an unconscious basis. But conflict, pain, and unresolved problems can become the source of chronic uneasiness, blocked growth, and even illness.

The complex body-mind can provide new steps. Our deepest bodily knowledge can be welcomed and then lived further. Focusing, whose steps are described with care and clarity, taps and articulates new subliminal knowing. It befriends and listens to "the body," a term Gendlin uses comprehensively to mean the total brain-mind environment as we sense it. (The shifts elicited by focusing, felt in the body, involve deeper brain structures as well.)

Focusing is at once richly complex and surprisingly simple. It is mental and kinesthetic, mysterious in its capacity to summon buried wisdom, holistic in its respect for the "felt sense" of a problem. An effective method in itself, it is also valuable in conjunction with a variety of psychotherapies, with biofeedback, with meditation, to unblock the creative process and define problems.

In short, focusing works for any form of "stuckness."

I first heard of focusing at a clinical conference in Chicago in 1977. Norman Don, a psychologist, reported on recent research in which he had wired up experienced focusers, then observed their brainwave patterns as they attempted to elicit a felt shift—Gendlin's term for the bodily change and sense of release that accompanies the sudden new understanding of a previously unclear feeling.

The brain's alpha and theta rhythm activity shifted just before the focusers signaled a felt shift. The patterns of subsequent electroencephalographic activity suggested "reorganization at a higher level of integration." I reported on Don's experiments in *Brain/Mind Bulletin*, in May 1977.

In April 1978 I saw the first half-dozen chapters of the *Focusing* manuscript. Curious to know more about the method and its physiology, I put my work aside and began to read.

I was first impressed by the easy, conversational tone of the book, the effort to convey the concept of focusing on a simple level. Then I became increasingly excited by the possibilities of the method. Following the instructions in the manuscript, I made my first tentative effort to focus—and hit paydirt! The process triggered an overwhelming personal insight, a sudden fusion of intellectual and "gut" knowing. This shift released a tension of which I had been only dimly aware. I felt oddly light and free, exhilarated, as if an old burden had been taken away. The felt shift marked the end of a year-long siege of migraine headaches.

I have since taught the rudiments of focusing to several people, including my children, in situations of unexpected stress. Although focusing is best pursued as a deliberate strategy over a period of time, it is also valuable as a kind of psychological first-aid, as useful to a distressed, "stuck" person as a tourniquet to an accident victim. And I have given *Focusing* to countless friends who feel blocked and are open to new tools.

Modern psychology maintains that we can sometimes solve our problems by tapping into materials below the surface of consciousness. New questions and answers seem to lie out of reach. Using and capturing unconscious knowledge has been a chancy, erratic business.

Focusing grew out of the observation by Gendlin and his co-workers that many people were not being helped by traditional therapy. Those greatly improved were distinctive in their ability to tap an internal process ignored by most clients. Gendlin determined to understand this process so it could be taught and used by anyone.

Focusing moves inward, drawing on information from the deeper, wiser self ("the body"). If the right steps come, usually within half a minute or so, the felt shift or bodily release occurs.

Interestingly, based on what we now know of how the brain's two cerebral hemispheres specialize in their mode of knowing, it appears that the phenomenon of the felt shift may actually reflect whole-brain knowing. That is, the brain's analytical left hemisphere, dominant for language, names that which heretofore was inarticulate and diffuse, known only to the holistic, mute right brain. New information seems to be mediated primarily by the right hemisphere, which is also more richly connected to the evolutionarily older limbic brain.

The emergence of a step forward on a problem, and the simultaneous physical sense of relief, suggest a sudden knowing in *both* hemispheres.

The felt shift is essentially identical to the freeing insight of the creative process. The spontaneously creative person has learned to pay attention to at first vague impressions that open into new meaning. Focusing improves scores on many measures of creativity. Gendlin has pointed out that most approaches to teaching creativity focus on the negative: how to let go of old beliefs. But there are few strategies for approaching the new. Focusing is such a method. It helps to make the implicit explicit. It draws fuzzy, preverbal knowledge into definition and expression.

Focusing is also optimistic. It sees the individual in terms of process, not pathology.

Focusing can foster major shifts. With these more profound changes, Gendlin said in an interview, a body shift sometimes occurs without the usual accompanying words, phrases or images. "A whole constellation is changing. The ideas are so new we don't yet have a way to talk about them."

Usually, he said, we react in accustomed ways, "repacking our experiences in the same old concepts, when what we need is to let something wider in." If the focuser stays with the bodily sense of the shifting constellation, eventually new language and new metaphors, appropriate to the fresh understanding, will emerge.

Focusing is no conventional repackaging of self-help wisdom. It is at once a manual and a philosophy. It talks about the body's wisdom, the steps of the focusing technique, how to discover the richness in others by learning to listen. It looks at the potential for a new kind of relationship and a new kind of society, transcending outmoded roles and patterns. "A new society is forming," Gendlin tells us, "one in which the individuals are much more developed and aware than has been true throughout history.... A society of pattern-makers is coming."

This book is about that society and about how we can ease its emergence by helping ourselves and each other.

Marilyn Ferguson
Los Angeles
November 1980

PART ONE

Unlocking the Wisdom of Your Body

Chapter 1
The Inner Act

At the University of Chicago and elsewhere in the past fifteen years, a group of colleagues and I have been studying some questions that most psychotherapists don't like to ask out loud. Why doesn't therapy succeed more often? Why does it so often fail to make a real difference in people's lives? In the rarer cases when it does succeed, what is it that those patients and therapists do? What is it that the majority *fail* to do?

Seeking answers, we studied many forms of therapy from classical approaches to recent ones. We analyzed literally thousands of therapist-patient sessions recorded on tape. Our series of studies had led to several findings, some very different from what we and most other professional therapists expected.

First, we found that the successful patient—the one who shows real and tangible change on psychological tests and in life—can be picked out fairly easily from recorded therapy sessions. What these rare patients do in their therapy hours is different from the others. The difference is so easy to spot that, once we had defined it, we were able to explain it to inexperienced young undergraduates, and they too were able to sort out the successful patients from the others.

What is this crucial difference? We found that it is not the therapist's technique—differences in methods of therapy seem to mean surprisingly little. Nor does the difference lie in what the patients talk about. The difference is in *how* they talk. And that is only an outward sign of the real difference: *what the successful patients do inside themselves.*

The purpose of this book is to tell you what they do and how you can do it. For this uncommon skill, this internal act, not only is useful in a psychotherapist's office, it is a way of approaching any problem or situation.

We have taught this skill to large numbers of people not in therapy in subsequent years. Now that it seems anyone can learn it, I also want this book to be readable by anyone. The book is addressed to professionals, but not only to them. Therefore I am writing it simply and not in the technical manner of my philosophical and scientific publications.

The skill we have observed and defined is not only for problems. Among those who know it, it becomes an internal source that is consulted many times every day. I am using it right now, in the process of writing this book.

The skill I am about to teach you is called *focusing*.

It will enable you to find *and change* where your life is stuck, cramped, hemmed in, slowed down. And it will enable *you* to change—to live from a deeper place than just your thoughts and feelings.

One fact that disturbed us the most in those research studies was that patients who did the crucial thing inside themselves could be picked out in the first two therapy sessions. We found we could predict success or failure right from the start just by analyzing the early interviews. According to a careful statistical analysis, there was less than a thousand-to-one chance of getting the same finding accidentally.

Today we know how to teach focusing. So this finding does *not* mean that some people cannot learn it. But at the time this was a shocking discovery. Here we had therapists and patients embarking on a year or more of hard effort. Much human need, hope, devotion, and money would be involved, and we already knew they would fail.

The finding means that psychotherapy as usually practiced doesn't show patients how to do psychotherapy. In other words, patients did not improve with practice. If they did not somehow know right from the start how to approach themselves inside in that special way, they did not achieve major changes, no matter what they or their therapists did or how earnestly or for how long.

This finding was contrary to my predictions, and to what had been my own firm subjective conviction. I *thought* I had *experienced* the gradual opening and increasing ability of patients to come into touch with their feelings. I had been certain that patients learn to do psychotherapy in themselves over the course of treatment, and do it more effectively in the second half. I had had many experiences of beginning with patients who seemed inept at sensing themselves inwardly, and, by my own skills as a therapist, and with the patients' efforts, I had brought many such patients to a successful resolution of their problems.

One reason why research is so important is precisely that it can surprise you and tell you that your subjective convictions are wrong. If research always found what we expected, there wouldn't be much point in doing research.

With hindsight I realize I was thinking only of the successful patients and not of the many patients with whom I failed. Now we know how to teach these people the crucial skill as well.

The research shows plainly, and repeatedly, that *successful* patients do indeed improve in this key skill, but the research also shows that they had it to some extent right at the beginning. The others, those who failed, did not have it at all and never achieved it through psychotherapy alone. At that time we did not know how to teach it.

Most therapists don't know what this crucial internal approach is, let alone how to help patients learn it. So I was led to wonder: can it be taught?

My first feeling, stemming from my training as a psychotherapist, was to say no, it can't be taught. I was trained to believe that only a very naive therapist would try to tell the patient in words how therapy works. Someone who hasn't experienced it wouldn't understand the words. Psychotherapy was supposed to be an art, a mystery, not a science. Some groups claim to have developed exact scientific techniques, but this is only a propaganda claim. The omniscient and totally self-assured psychotherapist exists only in the movies. Of course, each school of therapists has its own ideas and techniques, but they all know that they stumble around confusedly when their techniques don't work, which is more often than not. Therefore no serious psychotherapist would claim to be able to put into words exactly what makes therapy work, how to make changes happen inside a person. Only therapy itself was supposed to teach how.

But the research had shown that therapy does not teach how to those who don't already *know* how. The research had also shown very specifically what the crucial inner act is. Was it naive, now, to think it might be teachable?

Despite my doubts, I set out to see if I could make that all-important inner act teachable. With many people's help, I gradually devised specific directions for doing what those rare successful patients had somehow known how to do. We tried those directions out on large numbers of people and revised them and tried them again many times over a period of years. Those instructions have now become very specific and very teachable. Research conducted in several places has shown that people can be taught effectively in these ways to perform that internal act (see appendix).

Since this crucial internal act can be taught, and is not taught by therapy, people need not be therapy patients to learn it. What follows from this fact is a kind of revolution. No longer need this change process be in the charge of therapists. *People can do it for themselves and with each other.*

Of course they are not "therapists" or "doctors" or "authorities" with each other, but the authority aspect of the medical doctor never has really fitted the human process of personal change at all. Human problems are by their very nature such that we are each inherently in charge of ourselves. No authority can resolve our problems or tell us how to live. Therefore I and others have been teaching more and more people to help themselves and each other.

This book will let you experience and recognize when actual change is happening in you, and when it's not. There is a distinct physical sensation of change, which you recognize once you have experienced it. We call it a body shift. When people have this even once, they no longer helplessly wonder for years whether they are changing or not. Now they can be their own judges of that. Often, when focusing is taught to a new group, some people experience a bodily shift, a step toward resolution of a problem they have discussed with a therapist for many years without change. They are shocked. Could a few minutes of this let me experience more change than I've had in my expensive psychotherapy?

People still think of the therapist as an authority. Even if patients feel no change, they think "the doctor" must know what's happening. If "the doctor" thinks they should keep coming, they accept it as necessary. They think something "must be happening." As someone wrote me recently: "When I confronted my therapist about there being no change, he thought it was all right if I have a paid friend for the rest of my life. I never went back... but after four years!"

When the revolution in self-help fully takes place and people generally learn and do these helpful processes with each other, will professional psychotherapy be unnecessary? I think expert help will always be wanted. But it will have to be better than what ordinary people can do when trained in *specific* skills. People will know how to recognize, unmistakably, whether they are being helped or not.

One must try out a number of therapists (a few sessions at a time, not years!) in order to find real help. You can do this after you learn the unmistakable bodily experience of a bit of change going on.

My approach to therapy and some of my colleagues' approaches too have been radically changed by the knowledge that the crucial inner act is teachable. When people come to me for help, I no longer let them talk and talk. And of course I don't—and never did—just analyze their feelings intellectually. Nor do I let them scream the same phrases and work in circles on the same things over and over again as happens in some of the newer therapies. Many people can get in touch with feelings—but then what? They have "gut feelings" all right, but the feelings don't change.

Focusing is the next development after getting in touch with feelings. It concerns a different kind of inward attention to what is at first sensed *unclearly*. Then it comes into focus and, through the specific internal movements I am about to present, it changes in a bodily way.

Another major discovery is that the process of actually changing feels good. Effective working on one's problems is not self-torture. The change process we have discovered is natural to the body, and it feels that way in the body. The crucial move goes *beneath* the usual painful places to a bodily sensing that is at first unclear. The experience of something emerging from there feels like a relief and a coming alive.

From this new vantage point, the traditional methods of working on oneself are seen to have been mostly pain-centered. People get into and repeat over and over their painful emotions, without knowing how to use the body's own life-centered and inherently positive direction and force. That way people stay as they are and hurt themselves over and over. One of the chief new principles is that the change process *feels good*. It feels like inhaling fresh air after having been in a stuffy room for a long time. The moment it doesn't, you stop and back up just a little bit.

This crucial skill is not easy to explain. Many people can do it only after some practice. On the other hand, it is very much easier than struggling for years with the old troubles, perhaps ending with a better self-understanding but with no change, perhaps getting in touch with feelings but being unable to make them move, shift, resolve themselves.

As hard as it was for me at first to accept the research finding that therapy doesn't do the job, research findings can never hurt you. They move you forward. If the therapy as it now exists doesn't do the job, then we must change therapy.

The happiest change of all is that we can build the change process into society generally and not only in doctor-patient therapy that costs so much and sometimes gives so little. Now that the inner act is teachable, we can teach it not just to therapy patients but to anyone. We have found that it can be taught in a school system, in church groups, in community centers, in many other settings. Any person can use this internal process. People can also be shown very specific ways to help each other with it.

Before I start to explain this inner act, I want to make an earnest request of you. Put aside for a while what you know about psychotherapy or inward processes. What I am about to show you is not the familiar "getting in touch with feelings." Nor is it the content-free quiet of meditation. Whether you are a psychotherapist, patient, or intelligent layperson, this inner act is probably quite unfamiliar to you. The internal equipment needed to perform the act is in every human being, but in most people it is unused. A few seem to use it intuitively now and then, but the chances are you have never deliberately done it and have never been aware the possibility exists. Only recently is it being discussed in the professional literature.

Some people learn this inner way fairly fast, while others need some weeks or months of patient inner listening and tinkering.

Chapter 2
Change

The process I am going to teach you in this book, the inner act, is a perfectly natural one. But as our language contains no words to describe it, I have had to invent the needed words.

I call the process *focusing*. It is a process in which you make contact with a special kind of internal bodily awareness. I call this awareness a *felt sense*.

A felt sense is usually not just there, it must form. You have to know how to let it form by attending inside your body. When it comes, it is at first *unclear*, fuzzy. By certain steps it can come into focus and also change. A felt sense is the body's sense of a particular problem or situation.

A felt sense is not an emotion. We recognize emotions. We know when we are angry, or sad, or glad. A felt sense is something you do not at first recognize—it is vague and murky. It feels meaningful, but not known. It is a body-sense of meaning. When you learn how to focus, you will discover that the body finding its own way provides its own answers to many of your problems.

The process brings change.

A therapist is *not* necessary in focusing. By yourself, or with a friend who knows how and when to keep quiet, you can achieve focusing results.

The most important rule for a therapist or friend to observe, in helping someone to focus, is to stay out of the focuser's way. Most therapists like to believe it is they who produce results, rather than a process in the patient. Therapists have much to offer and think this will make all the difference. There is always a strong temptation to analyze what the patient says, to make guesses about the nature of the problem, to lecture, to rearrange the person's situation.

But only your body knows your problems and where their cruxes lie. If I were your personal therapist, I would resist the powerful temptation to tell you things, as though I knew more about your problems than you do. But I would not just let you talk either. I would teach you how to focus effectively, and I would keep you company as you did so. There are also some other things I would do, which I will tell you about later.

Now let me give you some examples of some people's focusing experiences.

Later I will carefully explain each of the six *movements* of which focusing consists. When these are successful, there is a physical change in the body, a felt shift. Then the problem seems different. In the following examples I am not yet teaching the focusing movements. I am only illustrating what the changes are like that come with each body shift.

Notice that the nature of the problem changes as each shift comes. Without tapping the deeper bodily level, which is at first always *unclear*, one would stay stuck with the thoughts and feelings of what the problem appears to be at the beginning.

The Young Woman Who Thought Death Would Be Peaceful

Fay phoned me in the middle of the afternoon. She had been walking through city streets all morning, with thoughts about suicide. "Life is too much trouble," she said, and she really felt the limits of weariness and despair. "What's the use of going on with it? Where does it get me?"

Fay had talked to me before and I knew about some of her life. She is an attractive woman of about twenty-eight. A few years ago she had broken up with a man for whom she had felt a lot of love—call him Ted. She had not loved a man before or since. Since Ted had left, she had spent time with a succession of other men, searching for another Ted but not finding one.

"What feels so bad?" I said. "Give yourself a peaceful minute and see what feels so bad."

Quicker than I would have liked, but after at least some time of silence, she said: "I didn't get my period. I'm scared I'm pregnant."

The last time she had talked to me she had told of being with a man whom she found dull, stuffy, insensitive, not interested in her as a person but only as a sex partner. She had spent a weekend with this man.

"I miss Ted so much!" she cried over the phone. "And now my period is late. What if I'm pregnant? Oh God, what's going to happen to me?"

I could sense that her agitated feelings were running off again. She was finding it hard to stay more peacefully with her attention lower down inside, as focusing requires. She was obsessed with painful emotions instead of trying to find that deeper place, the felt sense.

I asked her to begin with what I call the "first movement" of focusing. This is the act of pushing problems to one side temporarily, stacking them, stepping back and looking at them. In a way, this is something like coming into a room so cluttered with furniture and packing crates and bric-a-brac that there is nowhere to sit down. You push things around so as to clear a little space for yourself in one corner. Of course, you haven't emptied the room. The things that were in your way before, the problems, are still there. But at least, now, there is a space for you to be.

"Just stand back, now, and take each thing that's bad, and stash it in front of you. One by one. See what each thing is that *feels* bad."

She cleared her space. The two major problems she found herself looking at were that she wanted Ted back, and she feared she might be pregnant.

"Which one is the worst?" I said.

"It's missing Ted that hurts the most," she said, beginning to weep again. "The loneliness, not having anyone to turn to . . . it's no use. . . ."

Another agitated, self-destructive emotional spiral was beginning and I interrupted her. (In much the same way, when you learn to focus, you will learn to interrupt yourself.) "Why don't you go down inside there," I said, "and see what the worst of that is? Just stay quiet for a little while. Get to the unclear body sense of all of it."

She knew what to do. She had focused before. If you ask why, in that case, she needed me on the phone at all—why she hadn't simply sat down and focused herself—the answer is simply that it can help to have another person present, even if that other person is only a friendly voice on the phone. This is particularly true if, as in her case, you are caught in a trap of emotions and can't seem to get out. Often, when that happens, all that is needed is a friend's voice saying, "All right, let's just sit and be quiet for a while. . . ." A friend can interrupt an emotional spiral when you feel powerless to interrupt it yourself.

I listened to the silence on the phone as Fay went into the second movement of focusing. She was making contact with the feeling of "*all that* about Ted being gone." With her, as with most practiced focusers, these movements tended to flow into each other and become one, just as a practiced golfer or pole vaulter puts many separate body movements together into one fluid motion. Having gotten the felt sense, she sensed *the quality* of it and got a "handle" on it—a word that fitted the quality exactly. (Third movement.) Finally, she checked the words against the feeling and found them right.

"It's all about anger, or something," she said. "I don't know.... It's like I'm angry—at—Why would I be angry?"

She was asking herself or me for an intellectual analysis. I didn't offer one. Focusing avoids analyzing. I also tried to help her not go off on an analysis. I said, "Go back to the felt sense and ask it, see what the anger is."

Asking is the fifth movement of focusing. She asked the felt sense, directly, what the anger was about.

I heard her sigh as this happened. I knew something had shifted inside. To the focuser, a shift is a definite, physical feeling of something changing or moving within, a tight place loosening.

After another silence, she said, "I'm angry at myself. That's what it is. For sleeping with all those men I didn't love, didn't feel anything for." Analysis would not have produced this answer. Instead of being figured out, it had to come from the felt sense.

Back through the focusing movements again, waiting for another shift toward resolving the problem. It is a shift whenever the felt sense changes, even if just a little.

Then more silence and another step: "And part of it is,

I'm angry with myself for sleeping with Ralph, maybe getting myself in trouble—an abortion, maybe. And I call myself bad, also, sleeping with a man I don't care for." Another deep breath.

Sometimes a shift will seem to clarify what emerged from a previous shift, or to elaborate it. This is what happened just now, when she had found "And I call myself bad...," which continued from what came before. But then her next step changed the previous series. In focusing, one must take what comes. Often what is next for the body is not what would logically come next. This happens frequently in focusing. It is unpredictable and fascinating.

She said, "There's a kind of heavy discouraged feeling." And after a while this heavy discouraged feeling opened and the details came out. "It's about all these men I don't care for. I have no sexual feelings with them...."

She was silent for a while. I heard her say that word "discouraged" to herself, as though she were trying it out. Apparently it didn't quite match the feeling, for she sounded dissatisfied with it. She checked with the feeling again to see whether a more exact word would come up from it. She was trying to match a specific physical sensation.

This experience of Fay's is a common one in focusing. A change begins but seems oddly, mysteriously incomplete. It gives you the start of a shift, but you know (your body knows) a more complete shift is possible. You stay tuned to your bodily feeling and wait for it to happen.

Suddenly she said, "Weary!" The relief in her voice was clearly audible. The complete shift had taken place. "That's it. I'm weary. I feel like I'll spend the rest of my life going from one dull man to another, never feeling sexual but never letting myself stop trying. I can see all those men lined up ahead of me, all those blank faces, rows and rows of them from here to the end of my life. I'm condemned not to have sexual feelings, that's what."

I waited for her to say more. Evidently she felt that this focusing session had accomplished what she needed for the moment, for she suddenly said, "I feel better now. What a load to get rid of!"

Get rid of? To a rational observer, she had rid herself of nothing. The problems that had existed when she first phoned me, the problems that had driven her close to suicide, still existed. What had she really accomplished by focusing?

She had changed inside.

It had seemed a problem of loneliness. With the first shift it was her anger at herself, and with the next shift it was her calling herself bad. Then the heavy discouragement came up, and with a bodily release it turned out to be a conviction that she would never again have sexual feelings. Even as she sensed this last, it changed in her body.

At such a time one cannot yet know just how much change has happened. Many more cycles of focusing would be needed later. But a change happens in a body shift. Some change happens even in the mere bodily relief of sensing and touching the trouble in just one definite deep place.

When she first phoned me, her bad feelings were diffused throughout her body. Her whole body hurt. But now she had localized the problem and it had shifted. The rest of her body was released.

Focusing helped her in a time of desperation. In the following months she continued to focus and to change inside. Eventually her sexual life and some other painful aspects of her life became rewarding. By that time she had woven focusing into her way of living. It became more than a therapeutic tool to be used in times of crisis. It became something to be used every day, a comforting and familiar part of daily existence.

The Man Who Felt Inappropriate

Fred, as I'll call him, had an almost constant knot in his stomach, a tightness that never quite went away.

The stomach knot was worse on some days than on others. It was particularly bad on the day Fred first focused effectively.

The day had begun badly. He had had an argument with his boss.

Fred was an interesting man who had a job as a sales executive in a manufacturing company. The company wasn't doing as well as it had at one time. Fred believed he could fix that by reorganizing the sales force, and he had drawn up a detailed plan for doing so. This made Fred feel more creative on his job. The plan involved a fairly drastic change in the company's general selling philosophy, and this proposed change had pulled Fred into the argument with his boss.

The emotional residue of the argument settled in Fred's stomach and stayed there all day. After work that evening, he tried all those familiar approaches that don't work.

He tried lecturing himself: "Get hold of yourself! You let little things upset you too much. Rise above it! Stay cool!"

When the self-lecture was over Fred's stomach was still in a knot.

He tried reliving the argument, going round and round

with it: "When he said *this*, I should have said *that*." Of course, this only increased his emotional tension.

He tried the trick of pretending the problem didn't exist. "Nothing really happened at all," he told himself. "My boss knew my views long before this, and I knew his. The argument didn't change anything. It just got things out into the open, and that ought to make me feel good, not bad. Sure! I feel *good!*"

But his stomach didn't believe it. It was still in a knot.

He tried analysis. "He's an old-timer, wedded to old ways of doing things, scared of change. That's his hangup. My hangup is that I'm basically scared of older men in authority...."

His stomach didn't relax after that approach either. An analysis of a personal problem might be true. But it is different from going inside to feel directly how it is.

When all of Fred's attempts to make himself feel better failed, he went to a bar and had a couple of drinks. But this made him feel only a trifle better. He could still feel the same knot in his stomach, only the pain was slightly muffled because of the alcohol in his system.

Later that night, when the alcohol had worn off, he tried focusing. He had learned it from me a few weeks earlier but, so far, had been unable to do it well. Now he sat down on the edge of his bed and found himself able to do it.

This is what he reported:

"I made myself shut up inside, turned off (or at least turned down) all the lecturing and intellectualizing and other noises that had been thundering in my skull. I let my attention go down, not just to the argument with my boss but to get a feeling of all the thousands of details that surround it, all my concerns about my job and my future and what I am doing with my life."

This large, vague feeling is what I call a felt sense.

Then he sought the core of the felt sense. He stayed with the vague discomfort. "I asked myself what was the worst of it? Where did it hurt the most?

"I tried to grasp the quality of that. It was so strange I couldn't make it speak to me. It was a feeling of something being out of place. It was the kind of feeling you might get from seeing a picture hanging crooked on the wall, or a book placed upside-down in a bookcase, something not quite right.

"I waited for words and got 'out of place' and 'off,' but when I checked to see if they were right, they weren't—not quite. I felt very close, I had that tip-of-my-tongue feeling, the feeling I get watching a quiz show, and I *know* I know the answer but I can't quite bring it up.

"I never got that far with focusing before. I never had that feeling without knowing—the felt sense that you talk about all the time. This time I knew I had it.

"Then I got it, got my word. It was *inappropriate!*

"That was my word. And I did feel my knot, my tight place inside coming loose. And right away, I knew."

He had not needed to make a separate movement of *asking*. The body shift and release came along with the word.

Inappropriate: that was the word—as his body felt it—that described all his actions in his job: his elaborate plans for reorganizing the sales force, his arguing with his boss, everything. All were inappropriate, for this job wasn't what he really wanted to do with his life.

He had long thought he was past all his youthful dreams, thought he had "grown up" and become practical with maturity. But now, in that body shift, that feeling of a knot loosening inside, he knew something that came along with that one word "inappropriate." He knew it all in one instant flood.

What he knew was this:

"The reason I got so upset about the reorganization plan was that I was hoping for the plan to fix my life. And of course, that made me act stupid. What my life needs is much too big for that plan to fix. I didn't know that and it sure made me a difficult person to be with, on the job. It's like I was reacting with this enormous emotional intensity which doesn't fit the plan. My intensity was inappropriate to the plan, and I was acting inappropriately on the job.

"Of course, I sort of knew that I wanted the plan because then I could feel creative about my job. But I didn't know I was letting that plan be my whole life, the part of it I didn't manage to live out. No wonder I couldn't stay cool about it."

Fred hadn't known what he had invested in the plan, but his body knew. And all he needed to do was "ask" it.

Fred could never have figured this out analytically, partly because he thought he already knew his own answers. If someone had asked him to think it through, he might have answered that the plan made him feel like the creative person he wanted to be. And with this simple and true answer he would have prevented himself from coming into direct touch with the actual way the problem was

in his body. Also, Fred could not have figured this out analytically because his mind had been occupied with
thoughts about details and people on the job.

Fred tells this focusing story only as far as that evening
when the tightness in his stomach released. It is necessary
to observe, as with Fay, that Fred had not yet fully resolved
his problem in practical terms. But he would be detached
now, on his unwanted job, relaxed about the reorganization plan. He would certainly continue to champion his
plan because it was good, but he would be able to listen to
other people's objections and would be at ease in combin-
ing their ideas with his.

This relieved his immediate tension on the job. The
body shift had produced other changes as well. Something
had come free in him about changing his life. He puts it
this way:

"I could see that the job never could satisfy me even
if my plan or any number of plans got accepted, but
I felt better. I should have been discouraged. I certainly can't change my life just like that. It isn't as if I
hadn't thought about that before. But some way, this
element in me which needs something else got more
released, too. It was right there in me, some appetite
for living. I don't need to force it into a straitjacket
anymore. I don't know why, but it's there inside me,
a little excited thing, saying, We're going to change!
And I have no idea how, yet. If I were purely objective, I'd be discouraged."

Of course, to change his life took practical steps, not
only focusing. And it took more focusing to meet fears and

other obstacles inside, as well as practical steps outside. Fred didn't know at first what inner and outer changes would come to him to make. But since that time a whole new life has opened to him. As it turns out, he has been able to pursue his new interests without changing his job.

But that happened to be Fred's further development. Perhaps another person would have changed jobs. Still another might have found relief simply in not needing the reorganization plan to work out exactly as written. Focusing usually leads to deeper levels, but sometimes they are at peace and need no further change. In Fred's case, a new life direction began.

Previously, if he had been asked to apply a descriptive label to the job, he would have called it "this desperately important job that ties my stomach in knots." Now he could call it "this job that is only a small part of me."

Same job. Same man, but a man with an entirely new outlook on his goals in life, most immediately his job.

The Girl Who Was Scared of College

When I first saw Evelyn, she had come to Changes, a group of people in Chicago who welcome anyone. They practice focusing. They listen to each other, help each other in various ways.

Evelyn felt no purpose in life and had no goals. Nothing interested her. She had a part-time job but no idea of any work that would fit her.

She felt sexually exploited, without real sexual satisfaction in such relations as she had had. She was overweight, dull-eyed, and sad. She was also extremely quiet.

Some of the people from whom I have focusing reports,

or with whom I have done focusing, may seem to be quite hopeless when I first describe them. But focusing moves into the *inside* of a person. It discovers a richness there. Focusing will show you this in yourself and in others. Once you see it, nobody will seem hopeless. In fact, nobody will seem to be "a type," either, for these are only superficial and temporary aspects of people.

People coming to Changes show me this over and over. Someone who first strikes me as a certain kind of person—destroyed, hopeless, listless, boring—may later turn out to be different, rich, fascinating.

And so I remember my first impression of Evelyn. A woman named Lori had been listening to her regularly as she tried to focus, but Evelyn was hard to listen to. She never had any feelings at all. Evelyn could only talk about externals, situations, other people. It made her anxious that she had no feelings inside herself.

Several school and community therapists had tried to help Evelyn before without producing any notable results. In effect, without saying it in so many words, they had given up on her as hopeless.

Lori wasn't going to give up on Evelyn, and she sought help from another woman, Nancy. Between them they helped Evelyn realize that being anxious about having no feelings *was itself a feeling*.

They and others listened to Evelyn, and helped her to focus, fairly regularly for some months. For the sake of this book, I asked the Changes people to tape-record some of their sessions; Evelyn's was one. Evelyn gave me permission to reproduce a particular focusing session that made a major difference.

By the time this session took place, there was already a

different Evelyn. It had turned out, for instance, that she was bright, that she could differentiate her feelings with the precision of a thinker. There were all sorts of things in her that were the opposite of the woman she at first appeared to be. In that key focusing session she was concerned about her education.

"I guess I ought to go on to college," she said. "Everybody says I should, and I guess it's good advice. I mean, I know I have to if I want to do interesting work. But I just don't *want* to."

A pause, then: "The thing is, I'd have to give up everything else, and get a full-time job to pay for it, and—like, I'd never have just time to live. Everything would be tense, and—"

She interrupts herself. She knows she is just talking around the problem, repeating familiar reasons that have long been in her head. It is time to be silent to focus, and wait quietly to see what comes.

She sighs, and there is a long silence. Finally she says, "Well, all that about making a living and not having time, that isn't what it's about, not really." She starts to cry. "It's that it takes such a lot of faith, or something, to believe I could take that part of me seriously—I mean the thinking part, you know? The brain part, the creative . . . I want to be with thinking people, and I love reading and discussing and wondering about things, but to take this thinking part of me seriously. . . ."

She has achieved her first shift. Some tight place within her has come unstuck, and her crying is a tangible symptom of that release.

There is another pause, and then a second shift. As often happens in focusing, it is a change in direction, an adding-on of a new dimension. Verbally it can contradict what was said before.

"Well, it isn't exactly that. I mean, about taking this thinking part seriously. I could do it, but the thing is, school is just what's *in the way* of doing it. School would prevent me from doing it. That's why school was always so painful for me. Like I'm so unsure I can take me seriously, I need teachers to tell me my ideas are okay, I need thinking people to tell me, 'Yes, you're okay, you can think.' But teachers never do that. Nobody ever wanted this part of me at all. They always sent me off to do chores and other stuff *they* thought of, nonthinking stuff. So I had to force myself back inside myself, kind of. My thinking part had to stay hidden away because nobody wanted it. It was like I shouldn't come *out*. That's what going back to school feels like. It's that feeling of—you know, not letting myself out."

Between each cycle and the next there is a silence on the tape, in which she focuses. When there is a shift in the body's way of having the problem, then she speaks again. What she now says about the problem is different. She is silent again, focusing. But she doesn't work only on the problem as she just stated it. Instead, she focuses on the *whole sense* of discomfort, the new murky body-sense of what still feels unresolved. In this way she is not imprisoned within the thoughts and feelings of the problem as just stated.

Notice that what the problem seems to be about changes with each bodily shift. That is why it doesn't help much to try to solve a problem by working only on the thoughts and feelings one has about it at first.

She is crying again.

Then she has yet another shift. "It's not really what the teachers think. It's—well, this unsureness in me, this keeping myself from coming out. That's me. I mean, I'll go to college expecting a lot, and it will be the same as school always was, and I'll be disappointed and hurt all over again. I'll always be the same. Yeah, that's what the feeling is now. It's this feeling of . . . *that's not going to change.*" She sighs. She is silent for a time. Then another shift occurs.

"Ah, yeah, it's—it's not just that. This thing about not coming out—it isn't school. It's all the time. I've felt that way about me in almost everything. It's been there so long. . . ."

Another pause. She is listening inside again. Finally she says, "Yeah, it's like I keep myself inside because—because there is something I have to *not see.* If I come out, I'll see it. Yes, that's right." She cries for a long time. "I don't know what it is, but there is something I mustn't see, and if I come out I'll see it. No . . . people will see it, and I will see it. So I have to not see anything or hear anything. And I've always been, well, confused."

She cries again.

"I have to stay confused and not see . . . something. And I have to not come out so people won't see it."

There is a long silence as she focuses on the felt sense of that something. For a long time there is only silence on the tape. Some unknown *something* that she mustn't show people has made her keep herself locked inside. Some unknown thing that is wrong with her, something she has always tried not to see, not to run into. Trying not to run into that, she has kept herself from seeing or hearing anything at all too clearly. I know, although the tape is silent, that she is focusing on the unclear felt sense of *all that*—the whole felt sense of "something about me that I mustn't run into, that people mustn't see."

Then she cries again.

"Something is *wrong* with me! That's it—and people will see it if I come out." There has been still another shift.

"That's what it's all about," she goes on after a while. "It's an old feeling way down there, that something's terribly wrong with me. I don't know what it is . . . some terrible thing. So I have to be careful and not come out, because then people will see it, and I'll see it too."

So *that* was what her body really felt about going to college.

Suppose she hadn't focused and hadn't made contact with that place inside her. Suppose she had lectured herself, clenched her teeth, and forced herself to college despite all those inner doubts. With her body feeling that way, the college experience would have been awful. More likely, she would have continued to feel a barrier in her way, and now would have said that this was the way school always was. And, of course, that was true, but only part of a larger truth.

But now she was all right. The heavy, hurting place was localized. The rest of her body was released. And just because her body felt different, she (like Fred) was now able to take practical steps that would have been hard or impossible before, and to take them in a new way. The old felt sense would not have let her go to college and "come out," as she put it—would not have let her bring out that "thinking part" in a forceful, cheerful, confident way. But the old felt sense had changed. The changed sense not only let her go to college with hope and anticipation but enabled her to become interested in what she was doing once she was there. She had to work harder than other students because the coming-out issue was not resolved in one step. There were periods when she could not allow her love of thinking to show. But more and more her creative thinking ability came out, and she got to know and rely on it.

This could happen only through changes in the way her whole organism felt. Evelyn's story illustrates an important characteristic of focusing: You feel better, oddly, even when what emerges doesn't sound encouraging to anybody trying to analyze the situation rationally.

One effect of the focusing process is to bring hidden bits of personal knowledge up to the level of conscious awareness. This isn't the most important effect. The body shift, the change in a felt sense, is the heart of the process. But the bringing-up of bodily sensed knowledge—the "transfer" of this knowledge, in effect, from body to mind—is something that every focuser experiences. Often this transferred knowledge seems to be part of a tough problem, and it might be expected that this would make you feel worse. After all, you now know something bad that you didn't know before. Logically, you should feel worse. Yet you don't. You feel better.

You feel better mainly because your body feels better, more free, released. The whole body is alive in a less constricted way. You have localized a problem that had previously made your whole body feel bad. An immediate freeing feeling lets you know there is a body shift. It is the body having moved toward a solution.

There is also another reason. No matter how frightening or intractable a problem looks when it first comes to light, a focuser becomes used to the fact that at the very next shift it may be quite different. Nothing that feels bad is ever the last step.

For both reasons Evelyn felt better when she made

contact with a feeling that "some terrible thing" had always been wrong with her. To an analytic observer, this might seem like a nightmare: to stumble on the truth that you have kept yourself hidden for fear that some mysterious wrongness will come to light. But Evelyn felt better. She cried, certainly, but out of relief, and because the shut-in part of her was at last being heard. Crying is often the first stirring of a part of one's self that has been long held in. The body shift had felt good when she made contact with that feeling. Moreover, she was sure that further focusing would move that heavy place, just like others in the past.

When you are focusing well, you are glad about the coming of any feeling. You might hear an inner feeling say, "You're doomed!" You would consider this gently and understandingly. You would say, "Oh, that's interesting. A feeling of doom. No wonder I felt locked up—if there's been a feeling like that in there. Glad it came up. Let's find out where *that* feeling comes from." You can take this attitude because, many times before, you have experienced feelings like that changing and resolving themselves physically in a very few minutes.

Some months after Evelyn's taping session, at a large group meeting of Changes, there were some eighty people in the room. Sweeping my glance across the room, I saw a beautiful woman with bright, intensely alert eyes sitting somewhere in the middle. "Who is that?" I asked myself. "Someone new in the group?" Then I realized it was Evelyn! It had been only a few weeks since I had last seen her, but perhaps I had not looked closely at her for some time. I had been very aware of her intellectual sharpness. She had even helped me with a piece of writing. But I had never seen this!

When people change, they show it physically. At first this may not be outwardly noticeable, except in the momentary relaxation and easing of a body shift, the better circulation and deeper breathing. But over a longer period, with many shifts on different problems, it is definitely noticeable in the face, the carriage, the whole body. And it can be a startling change.

Later on, Evelyn traced the feeling of something wrong with her. It had come to her from her mother. She could then sense her mother's basic and constant attitude toward her: "Something's wrong with Evelyn. She isn't like anyone else." Evelyn discovered this with much relief and much crying, as her crowded-into-herself part at last became uncramped, and the big "felt block" shifted.

A postscript: Evelyn recently visited her parents. One evening her mother went out to attend one of a series of lectures on children. It turned out to be a lecture on exceptionally gifted children. Evelyn's mother came home excited, saying that the lecturer had described precisely what Evelyn was like as a little child. Her mother felt that—at last—she had discovered what had always been so odd about Evelyn.

The Man Who Couldn't Work

"I'm having a lot of trouble finishing this book I'm writing," said George. "It's because I have to do it. If I didn't have to, I could. But this way, I sit there and I'm sort of stuck—disconnected like. I can't seem to turn on my mind. All I do is sit there and stare out of the window. I can't do the actual writing. If I do have an idea, I sit there and sort of tell myself, 'Well, George, it's great that you have an idea here,' and then I feel like going and reading a mystery novel."

I said, "That body sense of 'stuck,' 'disconnected'— what is its quality? Focus on it."

He was silent for about a minute, sitting, eyes closed. He started to say something and then stopped: "It's a feeling of—no." Evidently he had a feeling and was trying to let words come from it. Words were coming, but when he checked them with the feeling, they weren't exactly the right words. They made nothing shift.

Suddenly, he had it: "Contempt!" He repeated the word, trying it again and liking it. "It's like this book isn't the real world, it's just in my head."

George is a college professor. He has a reputation for working harder with students than most professors do.

He went on: "This feeling of contempt—well, it's like everything I do sitting at my desk is crap. It's in my head, in my private space, instead of out in the world. That's what makes it crap. Head work isn't out in the world where things happen. It's all inside, like it isn't really happening at all. It isn't real or important. What's important is what I do in the world. That's real—teaching classes, seeing students, taking care of my family.... Ah, I've had this for years, off and on. Head work is nothing."

I repeated the gist of what he had said. "So there's in-your-head and that's contemptible," I said, "and there's in-the-world and that's real, that's taking care of things."

"Yes. No. Well—uh—"

This is what focusing is like. The nature of the problem changes with each shift. You make contact with a feeling and you say, "Yes that's it!" Then you feel something below it or behind it or alongside it and you say, "Well, no, that isn't it after all." The problem, when you finish, is not the same as you thought when you began. The *felt sense* of the problem changes.

George sat quietly for a while, focusing. Then he said, "There's something else here. It's crazy, paradoxical. This being in the world, taking care of things, it isn't the important part of me at all. Taking care of things, teaching, earning my salary—that isn't the main thing for me. I always arrange it so I can get it out of the way, get back to writing my book. It doesn't make sense, does it? Writing is contemptible because it's all in my head, but it's still the main thing, the thing I most want to do."

"What is the whole unclear body-sense when you say, 'this thing I most want to do'?"

"It feels like I have to do this writing. It dominates my life. It would be awful if I didn't do it, even though I have this contempt feeling about it."

I said, "All right, go back to it and say, 'Okay, right, it would be awful not to do this writing.' Then ask what that whole sense of 'awful' is."

George often goes past a feeling without letting a whole felt sense form. That is where I usually help. He knows it is important to accept every feeling that comes, not argue with it, not challenge it with peremptory demands that it explain itself. You don't talk back to the feeling like an angry parent demanding that the feeling justify itself. You don't say, "What do you *mean*, such-and-such would be awful? That's nonsense! Just why would it be awful?" Instead you approach the feeling in an accepting way.

George accepts his feelings, but this is not enough. Just getting in touch with one's feelings often brings no change, just the same feeling over and over. One must let a larger, wider, unclear felt sense form.

George had said "it would be awful." We didn't yet know what there was in and with this "awful." To find out, and to let it shift, the whole vague body sense of all that goes with "awful" had to form for him.

George focused on the felt sense and its quality. Then he said, "It would be awful not to write because—if I didn't do my book I'd be a failure, a parasite—well, no, not exactly that. . . ." He paused to let the right word come, and finally it did: "A playboy."

"A playboy. Now ask what that is."

"Ah. . ." George sat silent for a long time. "Yeah," he said at last, "yeah, this is a very evil path this leads me down. Wow. It feels—it feels like it's *immoral* not to do this serious work, writing." George breathed a huge sigh. "It's sexual," he said. "That's what it feels like. Not to have to work at writing: that's sexual. Like masturbating all the time, or—wait, no, it's more like being a kid watching adults making love. Yeah, that's what it would be like. It would be like having the grown-ups tell me I could just sit there and watch."

"And that would be all right?"

"Sure! That would be fine!" George's felt sense of the situation seemed to have given him permission to stop writing. But then that permission was withdrawn. "Wait a minute," he said. "I don't know if that would be fine after all. It would—well, ah, it feels both good and bad."

"Sort it out. See if you can get a felt sense of what would be bad about it."

"Well," he said after a while, "there's a feeling of blankness. Like, if I stopped writing I'd be facing a big blank. I'd have nothing to do but read mystery stories. I mean, if I didn't feel compelled to do this writing, I could do whatever I wanted—but I wouldn't find anything to do."

George had a "handle" word. If actually released from work, he'd get a "big blank." Because such an empty space is frightening, people who find one inside themselves often run back into work and other time-filling activities that they don't enjoy. Like Fred, the man with the knot in his stomach, they may drive themselves so hard to avoid the blank that they make themselves physically ill.

Focusing allows you to approach any such blank with equanimity, like anything else. For a blank is also a feeling. Instead of backing away from it in fear, you walk right up to it, and find out what is there.

I encouraged George to do just that. "Be with the body sense of that blank. What is its quality?" I asked.

George sat quietly, feeling around the emptiness. Then he said, "It feels like there are things I want to do, but—I'm *not allowed* to see them. Like when I was a kid, my father had certain books on the top shelf of a bookcase, and I wasn't allowed to look at them."

He paused again. I didn't push him. He asked into this sense of "not allowed." After a while he drew a deep breath and let it out noisily, and I knew something else had shifted inside. "Yeah," he said. "Yeah, of course. I'm an adult now, right? I can look at anything I want to look at. Sure, I— wait a minute.... Things are coming to me. Sure. One thing I'd do if I didn't have to work on this book—I'd jog. I've been wanting to go jogging but whenever I feel like it, I have to go and sit at my desk instead. Yeah, and—" He paused briefly while something else came up. "And I'd write a book about birth control! I've been wanting to do that for a long time. There's a point about birth control that nobody has ever brought out before, a really crucial point. I'd love to write that book! This book I'm stuck on now, it isn't anything I'm really excited about. But I can finish it too, I bet, if I let myself write what I want. This birth-control book—ah, that would be great!"

He paused for a long time. Then:

"Wow, yes, now this finishing this book is OK too. Yes, it feels all right. The point wasn't to finish the book, it was not to *have* to finish it. Under that have-to-but-can't feeling was all my good energy, all locked up. That's what I figured, all right, but I couldn't shift it. My whole life was under there, seems like. Letting myself have forbidden urges, yes, I see. To be free to stop, that's like being free to follow urges, and that's like being free to do what I want, which is to write. But free to write from out of my direct urge and energy. Well, I knew that all the time, but now I've got it."

George was analyzing now—in effect creating an intellectual rationalization to explain what his body had already solved. The analysis wasn't necessary. But intellectuals like to figure things out, and, done *in retrospect*, that's all right. What was important was that his body took its own steps first. Before these steps, his analysis wasn't effective.

Chapter 3
What the Body Knows

The stories in the previous chapter illustrate the two main discoveries on which this book is based:

First, that there is a kind of bodily awareness that profoundly influences our lives and that can help us reach personal goals. So little attention has been paid to this mode of awareness that there are no ready-made words to describe it, and I have had to coin my own term: *felt sense*.

And second, that a felt sense will shift if you approach it in the right way. It will change even as you are making contact with it. When your felt sense of a situation changes, *you change*—and, therefore, so does your life.

Let's study these two propositions in more detail.

First, I want to be sure you understand what a felt sense is.

A felt sense is not a mental experience but a physical one. *Physical.* A bodily awareness of a situation or person or event. An internal aura that encompasses everything you feel and know about the given subject at a given time—encompasses it and communicates it to you all at once rather than detail by detail. Think of it as a taste, if you like, or a great musical chord that makes you feel a powerful impact, a big round unclear feeling.

A felt sense doesn't come to you in the form of thoughts or words or other separate units, but as a single (though often puzzling and very complex) bodily feeling.

Since a felt sense doesn't communicate itself in words, it isn't easy to describe in words. It is an unfamiliar, deep-down level of awareness that psychotherapists (along with almost everybody else) have usually not found.

Let me illustrate. Think of two people who play a major role in your life. Any two people. I'll call them John and Helen in this discussion, but substitute the names of your own people.

Let your mind slide back and forth between these two people. Notice the inner aura that seems to come into existence when you let your attention dwell on John, the sense of "all about John." Notice the entirely different aura of Helen.

The inner aura as you think of each person isn't made up of discrete bits of data that you consciously add together in your mind. In thinking of Helen, you don't laboriously list all her physical and personal traits one by one. You don't think, "Oh yes, Helen: she's 5´6´´ tall, has blond hair and brown eyes and a small mole next to her ear, talks in a high voice, gets upset easily, wants to be a playwright, likes Chinese food, needs to lose weight...." Nor do you list each detail of your relationship with her.

There are undoubtedly millions of such bits of data that describe Helen as you know her, but these millions of bits aren't delivered to you one by one, as thoughts. Instead, they are given to you all at once, as *bodily felt*. The sense of "all about Helen"—including every one of those thousands of bits of data that you have seen, felt, lived, and stored over the years—comes to you all at once, as a single great aura sensed in your body.

The sense of "all about John" comes to you in the same way. It is a huge file of data: what John looks like, how he speaks, how you and he first met, what you need from him, what he said yesterday, and what you said in return. The amount of information is staggering—yet somehow, when you think of John, all the relevant facts and feelings come to you at once.

Where are all those thousands of items of information stored? Not in your mind, but in your body. The body is a biological computer,[1] generating these enormous collections of data and delivering them to you instantaneously when you call them up or when they are called up by some external event. Your thinking isn't capable of holding all those items of knowledge, nor of delivering them with such speed. It would take all the remaining years of your life to list all the details you know about Helen and your relationships to her. Your body, however, delivers "all about Helen" in one great, rich, complex experience of recognition, one whole felt sense.

To illustrate the point further, think of your own reactions when you talk with Helen, and then when you talk with John. You change inside—correct? You can *sense* the difference within you. If you are talking privately with Helen and then John unexpectedly walks into the room,

---

1. Ward Halstead, my colleague at the University of Chicago, spent a lifetime working on "biological intelligence." He devised many tests to measure bodily ways of discriminating different things: time, rhythms, spatial arrangements, interpersonal impressions, faces. When he read my book on "felt sense" he applied his term "biological computer" to it. The equivalent of hundreds of thousands of cognitive operations are done in a split second by the body.

you can feel yourself becoming different. Your felt sense of John is now here too, as well as your felt sense of Helen.

These changes inside you are not brought on by thinking. You don't think, "Oh yes, this is Helen: with her I've got to behave in such-and-such a way." Little thinking is involved. Ask yourself, "Why am I *this* way with Helen and *that* way with John?" The answers are not in your mind. Only your body knows.

Notice that a felt sense is not an emotion. It has emotional components in it, along with factual components. But it is bigger than any single emotion, more complex— and much less easy to describe in words.

For example, your felt sense of Helen probably includes a large number of emotions that you have felt at various times when with her. Perhaps some such emotion is dominant in your relationship at this very hour. The dominant emotion right now, let's say, is anger. You and she quarreled bitterly last night, and now the first word that comes to mind when you think of her is "anger." Yet that emotion is not the felt sense—is not "all about Helen."

An emotion is often sharp and clearly felt, and often comes with a handy label by which you can describe it: "anger," "fear," "love," and so on. A felt sense, being larger and more complicated, is almost always unclear—at least until you focus on it—and almost never comes with a convenient label.

To illustrate, let's suppose there is some difficulty in your relationship to John. Asked to describe this difficulty, you might say: "I'm tense when I'm with him. When I'm with Helen, I feel as if my 'natural' self is alive and free, but when I'm with John, I am uncomfortable, tense."

This tension arises somewhere in "all about John."

People who don't know about focusing are likely to be aware only of the tension, over and over. They never consult their felt sense of "all about John," or perhaps a little less broadly, "all about this odd feeling I get with John." The word "tense" might be the best one-word description of the feeling, but "tense" is only the tip of the iceberg. "Tense" might be the dominant emotion at a given moment, but below it and behind it lies something huge and vague.

You can feel that huge, vague something with your body, but you can't touch it with your mind—your mind protests, "I don't *want* to be struck dumb every time I'm with John! I want to be relaxed, bright, natural. Why can't I be? Why?" But there are no answers in your mind. If your mind knew the answers or had control of the situation, presumably you could surmount the difficulty through rational processes and an effort of will. You could think your way to a resolution of the problem. But this is patently impossible. No matter how your mind protests, no matter how hard you think, the same tension makes itself felt inside you whenever you are with John. This tension is generated by your body, reacting to John's presence. The reaction bypasses your thinking mind almost entirely. But when you let the felt sense form, then you can work with more than you can understand. If you attend to the felt sense through certain steps I will show you, it will shift.

That is precisely what this book is about. It is necessary to approach our felt senses by an entirely different route—that special through-the-body route that I call focusing. By approaching them that way, *we can let a felt sense form and change.*

Much of what has passed for emotional guidance and psychotherapy in our past has been futile. Counselors tried to make us analyze our feelings rationally, or "face" them over and over.

Let's look again at that hypothetical difficulty in your relationships with John, and let's look at some of the most common ways of approaching such a problem. (All the common approaches are, unfortunately, futile.)

Belittling the problem You try to convince yourself that the problem doesn't exist or is too trivial to worry about. "It doesn't matter," you tell yourself. "It's nothing. I shouldn't let such silly little things bother me."

Does this change anything? No. The next time you meet John, the "trivial" problem is exactly as big as it always was.

Analyzing "It must be that John reminds me of my father," you conclude solemnly. "I was always intimidated by my father. He was so sure of himself. So is John. Sure, sure, that must be it...."

The analysis may or may not be correct. But it does nothing to change the feeling. You can analyze furiously the whole time you are with John, but if that feeling is there in your gut with its inexplicable discomforts and tensions, the relationship will not be eased any more than it was last time.

"Facing down" the feeling "I'll just grit my teeth, stand up to it, and walk through it," you tell yourself hopefully. "I'll ignore it. I *won't* let it get me!"

But it doesn't help, does it? If something gets you, it will go on getting you until some fundamental change takes place.

Lecturing yourself "Now see here," you tell yourself sternly, "it's time you pulled yourself together and stopped all this nonsense. You're supposed to be an adult, right? So act like one! There's no reason in the world why John should make you feel uncomfortable...."

No. That doesn't work either.

Drowning in the feeling You sink into the emotion, hoping that this time just feeling it again will change it. "Yeah, that was a bad time when he started talking about my sex life. I just sat there like a dummy. I *am* stupid. Wow, that is awful! I feel like a squashed bug...." Whenever you sink into this unchanged feeling, it makes you feel as bad as last time.

These approaches cannot work because they don't touch and change the place out of which the discomfort arises. It exists in the body. It is physical. If you want to change it, you must introduce a process of change that is also physical. That process is focusing.

Part Two of this book devotes itself to the job of teaching you how to focus. I won't start teaching it here. For now, I just want to finish describing the characteristics of a felt sense.

The most exciting characteristic of all is the fact that a felt sense, when you focus on it well, has the power to change.

You can actually feel this change happening in your body. It is a well-defined physical sensation of something moving or shifting. It is invariably a pleasant sensation: a feeling of something coming unstuck or uncramped.

I can best describe it to you by starting with a familiar human experience: the odd feeling of knowing you have forgotten something but not knowing what it is. Undoubtedly it has happened to you more than once. You are about to take a plane trip, let's say, to visit family or friends. You board the airplane with a small, insistent thought nagging you: you have forgotten something. The plane takes off. You stare out the window, going through various things in your mind, seeking that elusive little piece of knowledge. What did I forget? What *was* it?

You are troubled by the *felt sense* of some unresolved situation, something left undone, something left behind. Notice that you don't have factual data. You have an inner aura, an internal taste. *Your body knows but you don't.*

Maybe you try to argue it away, try to squash it intellectually or rise above it—the method of belittling it. You tell yourself: no, I won't let this bother me and spoil my trip.

Of course, that doesn't work. The feeling is still there.

You sigh and rummage in your mind again. You find a possibility. "Helen's party! I forgot to tell Helen I can't come to her party!"

This idea doesn't satisfy the feeling. It is perfectly true that you forgot to tell Helen you would miss her party, but your body knows it isn't this that has been nagging you all morning. You still don't know what you forgot, and you still feel that wordless discomfort. Your body knows you have forgotten something else, and it knows what that something is. That is how you can tell it isn't Helen's party.

At some moments the felt sense of what it is gets so vague that it almost disappears, but at other moments it comes in so strongly that you feel you almost know. Then suddenly, from this felt sense, it bursts to the surface. The snapshots! I forgot to pack the pictures I was going to show Charlie!

You have hit it, and the act of hitting it gives you a sense of sudden physical relief. Somewhere in your body, something releases, some tight thing lets go. You feel it all through you: Whew!

It feels good. You may feel bad about the pictures but the step feels good. This is one of the key characteristics of a shift in a felt sense: it always has that easing and sometimes very beautiful sensation of bodily release. It feels like exhaling after holding your breath. You can feel the tension draining out of your body.

There are no words in the language to describe the felt sense and its physical shifts. Therefore, I must give a name to that feeling of coming unstuck inside. I call it the *body shift*.

Not everybody feels the shift taking place specifically in the belly. It may seem to happen all over the body, or it might feel like a loosening in the chest, or it might be a relaxation of a tight throat. I call it body shift mainly to suggest that it doesn't happen in the mind. It is always, in some way, a physical sensation. You often can see it and hear it when it happens in somebody else. There may be a long audible sigh of relief, a sudden loosening of some tight facial grimace, a quick, comfortable relaxing in the posture.

That is what it is like to get a shift in a felt sense. The example I've used—forgetting something on a trip—is trivial, of course. But undoubtedly there are problems in your life that you don't consider trivial. Stuck places inside you that spoil parts of your life, ways in which you feel trapped and helpless. In all these cases, exactly as with those forgotten snapshots, your body knows much that you don't know, much that you cannot possibly figure out.

Nobody can figure out, intellectually, all the details of a personal problem. No therapist can. You can't—neither for someone else nor for yourself. The details are in your body. The way to find them is through focusing.

When you do, as we've seen, a physically felt shift occurs. Why does it occur? Where does that odd feeling of release come from?

It comes from two sources:

First, the once-hidden knowledge is now available to your conscious mind. You may be able to use it in some rational plan of action for resolving the problem. This can certainly lead to a feeling of relief: "Yes, of course! *That's* where the hangup is.... *That's* the direction I need to go!"

The second source of that "uncramping" feeling is more important. Even if you can't make immediate or direct use of the once-hidden knowledge, the body shift makes your whole body different.

Consider those snapshots again. The once-obscured fact—"I forgot the snapshots"—was not the kind of fact that could be put to immediate use in a rational plan of action. The fact came to you aboard an airplane. There was nothing you could *do* with it. Despite this, your felt sense of your trip was now changed. *You* were changed.

And so it is with more important personal problems. You can *feel* the change happening inside you.

PART TWO

Focusing

Chapter 4
The Focusing Manual

The time has come for you to learn focusing.

The inner act of focusing can be broken down into six main subacts or movements. As you gain more practice, you won't need to think of these as six separate parts of the process. To think of them as separate movements makes the process seem more mechanical than it is—or will be, for you, later. I have subdivided the process in this way because I've learned from years of experimenting that this is an effective way to teach focusing to people who have never tried it before.

Think of this chapter as only the basic manual. As the book progresses we will add to these basic instructions, clarify them, approach them from other angles. Eventually—perhaps not the first time you go through it— you will have the experience of something shifting inside.

I'll start by giving you the focusing instructions in brief form, manual style. In the next chapter we will go through the six movements in a more detailed way, stopping to explain and elaborate.

Focusing Manual

1. **Clearing a space** What I will ask you to do will be silent, just to yourself. Take a moment just to relax. . . . All right—now, inside you, I would like you to pay

attention inwardly, in your body, perhaps in your stomach or chest. Now see what comes *there* when you ask, "How is my life going? What is the main thing for me right now?" Sense within your body. Let the answers come slowly from this sensing. When some concern comes, DO NOT GO INSIDE IT. Stand back, say "Yes, that's there. I can feel that, there." Let there be a little space between you and that. Then ask what else you feel. Wait again, and sense. Usually there are several things.

2. **Felt sense** From among what came, select one personal problem to focus on. DO NOT GO INSIDE IT. Stand back from it.

   Of course, there are many parts to that one thing you are thinking about—too many to think of each one alone. But you can *feel* all of these things together. Pay attention there where you usually feel things, and in there you can get a sense of what *all of the problem* feels like. Let yourself feel the unclear sense of *all of that.*

3. **Handle** What is the quality of this unclear felt sense? Let a word, a phrase, or an image come up from the felt sense itself. It might be a quality-word, like *tight, sticky, scary, stuck, heavy, jumpy*, or a phrase, or an image. Stay with the quality of the felt sense till something fits it just right.

4. **Resonating** Go back and forth between the felt sense and the word (phrase, or image). Check how they resonate with each other. See if there is a little bodily signal that lets you know there is a fit. To do it, you have to have the felt sense there again, as well as the word. Let the felt sense change, if it does, and also the word

or picture, until they feel just right in capturing the quality of the felt sense.

5. **Asking** Now ask: What is it, about this whole problem, that makes this quality (which you have just named or pictured)?

   Make sure the quality is sensed again, freshly, vividly (not just remembered from before). When it is here again, tap it, touch it, be with it, asking, "What makes the whole problem so _____?" Or you ask, "What is in *this* sense?"

   If you get a quick answer without a shift in the felt sense, just let that kind of answer go by. Return your attention to your body and freshly find the felt sense again. Then ask it again.

   Be with the felt sense till something comes along with a shift, a slight "give" or release.

6. **Receiving** Receive whatever comes with a shift in a friendly way. Stay with it a while, even if it is only a slight release. Whatever comes, this is only one shift; there will be others. You will probably continue after a little while, but stay here for a few moments.

   IF DURING THESE INSTRUCTIONS SOMEWHERE YOU HAVE SPENT A LITTLE WHILE SENSING AND TOUCHING AN UNCLEAR HOLISTIC BODY SENSE OF THIS PROBLEM, THEN YOU HAVE FOCUSED. It doesn't matter whether the body shift came or not. It comes on its own. We don't control that.

The Story of a "Trivial Problem"

Let's see the focusing movements in operation.

The woman who reported this experience is in her late

twenties. I will call her Peggy. She and her husband—call him John—live in a suburb. He works for a bank, where he has a real chance to become an executive. Peggy works part time as a teacher at the junior high school. The part-time status is necessary because she has to care for a five-year-old son.

One evening, John came home jubilant. The bank president had told him quite plainly that the bank had some expansion plans and that he, John, was considered a key element in those plans. In his excitement while telling Peggy of this, John knocked a dish off the kitchen table and broke it. It was her best china. Peggy flew into a sudden rage, ran upstairs in tears, and refused to cook dinner.

She was surprised and upset by her own outburst. Stormy scenes were not usual for her.

She sat alone in the bedroom and tried to patch herself up inside, using all those familiar approaches that we all use and that seldom work. At first she tried to dismiss the problem as "trivial," as though hoping she could belittle it out of existence. "So he broke an expensive dish," she told herself angrily. "Am I so dumb that I can be upset by *that?* The damned dish isn't all that important in my life. It's replaceable anyway. . . ."

That didn't work. The upset feeling refused to let itself be thought to extinction. Peggy next tried figuring it out. "Well, I've been under a lot of strain the past few days," she told herself. "I let the schoolwork pile up on me, had to stay up late grading all those papers. Haven't had enough sleep. . . . Sure, that must be it. No wonder I'm edgy."

No results. What Peggy told herself might have been

true, but nothing changed inside. The angry, irritated feeling stayed right where it was.

Finally she decided to try focusing. She had practiced it for several years and was very good at it—was, in a sense, "fluent" in it as one might be fluent in a familiar language. She didn't work her way through the six focusing movements one by one, as a beginner must do, but flowed through them in a single continuous movement. In re-creating her experience here, however, I will flag the various movements so that you can see how she got from place to place.

Preparation She began by getting as comfortable as possible, removing all unnecessary physical irritations that might have masked what her body wanted to tell her. She washed her face because it felt hot and itchy after crying. She took off her shoes, propped a pillow against the headboard of the bed, and leaned back against it.

First Movement: Making a space She stacked all her problems to one side, as though making a space for herself in a jumbled storage room. "Why don't I feel terrific right now? Well, there's that big pile of dog-eared school papers I still have to finish. And there's that problem about Jeff getting sent home from kindergarten. And of course there's this lousy new thing about the broken dish...."

She pushed all these problems a little distance away from her. She knew she couldn't make them go away. But she also knew, being a practiced focuser, that she could give herself a little quiet time away from them.

Second Movement: The felt sense Now she let her attention go to the problem that, at that moment, seemed to be the worst: the stormy scene involving that broken dish. She deliberately avoided trying to *decide* anything about it, trying to analyze it, figure it out. She simply groped for the felt sense of it.

She asked, "What does *all that* feel like?" And then she let the unclear sense come to her in its own way—large, vague, formless at first, lacking words to describe it, lacking labels or identifying marks of any kind.

She wasn't impatient with this formlessness. She didn't demand that it identify itself. Nor did she try to force an identification upon it: "Oh yes, of course, this odd feeling must be..." She simply let it exist in its own way for an appreciable time, perhaps half a minute.

Third Movement: Finding a handle Now, very gently, she asked what the quality of the felt sense was. She tried to let the felt sense name itself, or to let an image come and fit it.

Again she avoided analysis, avoided self-lectures, avoided assumptions and deductions. She wanted the answer to float up from the feeling itself, not from the confused clutter of material in her mind.

In the third movement a word, phrase, or image—if it fits exactly—provides a "handle" on the felt sense. One can then often feel the first shift, the first bit of internal movement (sometimes just a twinge of movement) that says *this is right*.

As often happens, she went through the focusing movements almost simultaneously here. She got a word (third movement), checked it (fourth), and asked the felt sense what it was (fifth).

Using more words than she herself did, I would put it like this. She had asked: "What is the worst of this?" The feeling came back: "Anger at John." A further question: "Over the broken dish?" The wordless reply: "No. The dish has hardly anything to do with it. The anger is over his air of jubilation, the way he radiates confidence about his future."

Thus did the problem change. The inner shift was unmistakable.

She received this fully and sensed it over and over, feeling the change going on in her body. When her body had finished changing, she went on.

A shift like this can come at any time in focusing. You receive it and continue another round of focusing.

Again she got the felt sense, now the changed way the whole problem was in her body at this moment. "His jubilation... what now is the *whole* sense of that?"

She waited. She did not try to force words onto the felt sense. She sat patiently and let the felt sense speak for itself (a second movement, again).

She tried to sense its quality, the fuzzy discomfort of the whole thing, and to get a "handle" on that quality (third movement again).

A word came: "Jealous."

Fourth Movement: Resonating She took the word "jealous" and checked it against the felt sense. "Jealous, is that the right word? Is that what this sense is?" The felt sense and the word apparently were a close match, but not a perfect one. It seemed that the felt sense said, "This isn't exactly jealousy. There's jealousy in it somewhere, but..."

She tried "sort-of-jealous" and got a tiny movement and the breath that let her know that was right enough, as a handle on the felt sense. She did it again, and... yes.

Fifth Movement: Asking Now she asked the felt sense itself: "What is this sort-of-jealous? What about the whole problem makes this sort-of-jealous?"

She let the question reach the unclear felt sense, and it stirred slightly. "What is *that?*" she asked, almost wordlessly.

And then, abruptly, the shift came. "Sort-of-jealous... uh... it's more like... a feeling of *being left behind*."

"Ah!" That "ah!" came with a large, satisfying sense of movement. Peggy's body was telling her that she was unhappy over the fact that her own career was stalled.

Sixth Movement: Receiving As she tried to stay with the relief of this shift, she had to protect it from voices that soon attacked her. "You shouldn't feel that way." "You're lucky to have the teaching job." And also, "How will you ever get your career moving?" "You know there's nothing you can do about it."

Peggy shoved all those voices over to one side. "That all has to wait," she said. And she came back to sensing the new opening. "Being left behind... can I still feel that?... Oh yes. There it is again, yes... that's right... that *is* how I feel."

Going Another Round

But this quality—the feeling of being left behind—was only the tip of the iceberg. Peggy wanted to see if it could lead to more change and movement.

And so she went back through the cycle of focusing movements again. "What *is* this left-behind feeling? What's really in it for me? What's the worst of it?"

This focusing session lasted for perhaps twenty minutes. When it was over, Peggy felt enormously refreshed. The shape of her problem had changed, and so *she* had changed. She and John then talked calmly about their lives and their futures.

The broken dish was forgotten. That one focusing session had not made Peggy's career-versus-motherhood problem vanish, but it had started a series of beneficial changes inside her. Further sessions told her more about herself and helped her to move from where she was stuck.

Chapter 5
The Six Focusing Movements and What They Mean

Now we will go through the movements more slowly. After you have read this chapter, try to focus on a personal problem and see if it works for you. Keep the book open to the Focusing Manual (Chapter 4) and take yourself unhurriedly through the six movements, paying special attention to the way your body feels at each stage of the process. If you feel no change, no shifts, go ahead to other chapters of the book and then come back and try again later. Eventually you will find yourself performing the inner act of focusing and the more often you do it, the easier and more natural it will seem (later on, use the Short Form at the end of the book).

Preparation

Find a time and a place to sit quietly for a while. If you want a friend to sit with you, that is fine and may actually help. But the friend must be content simply to listen quietly, must not expect you to speak if you don't feel like it, and must offer no analyses or assessments if you do choose to say what's inside you. Total silence is fine, and it is also all right for the friend to use words such as "Yes, I hear...I understand." But at this early stage, the friend must not say anything else.

It is a good idea to sit in some location that is at least slightly unfamiliar. That is, don't try to focus while sitting at the desk where you work, nor while sitting in your favorite armchair. Sit in another chair, or on the edge of your bed. Or, if you prefer, go out and walk or lean against a tree.

Try to find a sense of general physical comfort, if not total well-being. (That, with luck, will come later.) If small physical irritations are plaguing you, they will obscure other things your body is trying to tell you. If you are cold, put on a sweater. If your foot itches, take off your shoe and scratch. Settle back and mentally relax.

First Movement: Clearing a Space

Now ask yourself, "How do I feel? Why don't I feel wonderful right now? What is bugging me on this particular day?"

Stay quiet. Listen. Let what comes come. On any given day you are likely to find that perhaps half a dozen problems keep you tense inside. Some may be major life problems that you have wrestled with many times before. Everybody carries some such list around from one year to the next, and on any particular day one or two such problem areas will seem to be uppermost. Do not try to list every problem you can think of, but only what has you tense now.

Along with major personal problems, you are also likely to find that some relatively trivial ones are upsetting your tranquillity at a given moment.

Let all these problems come up and out: everything that is keeping you from feeling absolutely content right now. DON'T GET SNAGGED ON ANY ONE PROBLEM. Just list the problems mentally, the big and the small, the major and the trivial together. Stack them in front of you and step back and survey them from a distance.

Stay cheerfully detached from them as much as you can. "Well, except for all of these, I'm fine," you can now say. It might be an awful list but that *is* all. "There's that business about George and Joanne. And there's that loneliness thing—yeah, I know that one well, that's an old one. And there's that funny little one about what I said to Chris yesterday."

Do you feel a small increase of well-being in you? Keep stacking the problems until you hear something say, "Yes, except for those I'm fine."

Second Movement: Felt Sense of the Problem

Ask which problem feels the worst right now. Ask which one hurts the most, feels the heaviest, the biggest, the sharpest, the most prickly or clammy or sticky—the one that feels *bad* in whatever way you and your body define "bad." Or just choose one problem.

Now, don't go inside the problem as you usually would. Stand back from it and sense how it makes you feel in your body when you think of it as a whole just for a moment. Ask, "What does this whole problem feel like?" But don't answer in words. Feel the problem *whole*, the sense of *all that*.

In this second movement you will probably begin to encounter a lot of static from your mind: self-lectures, analytic theories, clichés, much squawking and jabbering. Somehow you must get down past all that noise to the felt sense underneath.

It is partly a matter of getting yourself to shut up for a change, and listen, and feel. You can get good results by being patient. Let's suppose the problem you are trying to focus on has to do with the souring of a once good relationship. As you try to feel the whole inner aura of the problem, the self-lectures may begin: "Here I go again, screwing up another good relationship. What's the matter with me? No matter how good it is, I'll always find some dumb way to make it bad."

When that kind of noise begins, turn it off tolerantly and gently. Tell yourself, "Yes, yes, I know all that. I'll listen some other time, if you like. Let's set it aside for now."

Be just as firm and polite if you find yourself trying to analyze the problem or trying to decide where the main drive of it lies. "Well, it's obvious what's gone wrong," you'll hear yourself say. "I'm basically scared of other people, so to cover it up I put on this big show. Like the other night when I..." Turn it off. Tell yourself, "Sure, you may be right about that. But right now we aren't trying to figure anything out. What we're trying to get at is *what does this whole thing feel like?*"

You are trying to get down to the single feeling that encompasses "*all that* about my relationships with..." or "*all that* about quitting my job." The feeling contains many details, just as a piece of music contains many notes. A symphony, for instance, may last an hour or more and contain thousands of separate musical tones, sounded by many diverse instruments, in a multitude of combinations and progressions. But you don't need to know all these details of its structure in order to feel it. If it is a symphony you know well, you only need hear its name mentioned and feel the aura of it instantly. *That* symphony: the feel of it comes to you whole, without details.

You are trying to make contact with the felt sense of a problem in the same way. Let your sensing go inwardly down past all the details that can distract and sidetrack you, past all the squawking and jabbering, *until you feel the single great aura that encloses all of it.*

No, it isn't easy—not at first. It is partly a matter of knowing what to pay attention to, what to ignore. It is a matter of knowing how to set your mind so that it will be receptive to certain things happening inside but not to others.

In seeking the felt sense of a problem, you are trying to make your mind do essentially what it does when calling up the feeling of your sense of a person. You may be aware of certain details but not snagged on them. Your attention is mainly on the single feeling, the sense of *all that.*

Once you have the feel of the whole problem, stay with it for a while. Don't try to decide what is important about it. Don't try to decide anything. Just let it be, and be felt.

The felt sense is the holistic, unclear sense of the whole thing. It is something most people would pass by, because it is murky, fuzzy, vague. When you first stay with it, you might think, "Oh, *that?* You want me to stay with *that?* But that's just an uncomfortable nothing!" Yes, that is just how your body senses this problem, and at first that's quite fuzzy.

Third Movement: Finding a Handle

What is the *quality* of the felt sense? Find a quality-word like "sticky," "heavy," "jumpy," "helpless," "tight," "burdened," or some word of that sort. Or a short phrase might fit: "like in a box," "have to perform." A combination of words might fit best, for example "scared-tight" or "jumpy-restless." Or a picture might pop up, which might get it best—for example, "a heavy leaden ball."

You aren't asking for analysis. What you are after is the core of the felt sense. You want the crux of *all that*, the special quality that comes up from it.

This quality may be a sense of having acted inappropriately, for example, or a sense of helplessness. Or it may feel oppressive, scary, tense, or uneasy—or there may be no word for it.

Once again, avoid forcing words into the felt sense. Let it come to you with its own essence. Or try one word gently.

In this third movement you may begin to find your problem changing. It may begin to feel different from what you expected before you started focusing: different from anything you might have figured out by rational means. The difference may be small and subtle and perhaps puzzling at first.

This is what you are looking for: something that comes along with a body shift. Discard everything else.

When a word or picture is right, we call it a "handle." As you say the words (or as you picture the image), the whole felt sense stirs just slightly and eases a little. This is a signal, as if it said: "This is right," just as in remembering something you forgot. The feeling of what you'd forgotten guides your remembering. You know that any number of perfectly sensible ideas are not part of the feeling, and you just drop them, until you get something the feeling itself opens up into.

It is like the old children's game of hide-and-seek. Someone who knows where the object of the search is hidden says "cold, colder, ice cold" when you move in the wrong direction, and "warm, warmer, still warmer" as you move in the right direction.

In this case it isn't another person but your own felt sense that will say "cold, cold, cold" (by not changing one bit) and then say "ah...warmer...hot! hot!" (by releasing, or shifting just slightly in how your body feels it).

Let words or pictures come from the feeling. Let it label itself: "scared," or "a stiff place inside me," or "a heavy feeling here."

Usually, finding the right handle gives one only a small bodily shift, just enough so you can tell the handle is right. You will have to sense for this small shift, so that you don't miss it. Your attention has to be in your body, to sense if this word, phrase, or picture makes that little relief in there that says, "It's right. It fits."

Fourth Movement: Resonating Handle and Felt Sense

Take the word or image you got from the third movement and check it against the felt sense. Make sure they click precisely into place—a perfect fit. Ask (but don't answer): "Is that right?"

There should be a felt response, some deep breath inside, some felt release again, letting you know that the words are right.

Sometimes, instead, this confirming sensation—this feeling of *just right*—doesn't come. Then try to sense more accurately. Wait again and let more exact words come from the feeling.

To do this resonating, you must experience the felt sense again. You must touch it again as a feeling. Many people keep hold of a felt sense quite well until they get the very first words for it. Then, somehow, the feeling disappears and they have only the words. If that happens, obviously you cannot check the words against the feeling directly. So you must let the felt sense come back—not necessarily the same feeling as it was, but the felt sense as it now is (perhaps a little changed). You say the words to yourself *gently* over and over, in the spirit of trying to feel directly what the words were about. Usually, after ten or twenty seconds, the feeling—as it is—is back.

It is all right if, of its own accord, the feeling changes, too, as you perform this matching procedure. Let both sides—the feeling and the words—do whatever they do, until they match just right.

When you get a perfect match, the words being just right for the feeling, let yourself feel that for a minute. You may feel impelled to say something like "Yes...oh yes...that's right..." and just allow it to *be*.

It's important to spend this minute. The sense of rightness is not only a check of the handle. It is your body just now changing. As long as it is still changing, releasing, processing, moving, let it do that. Give it the minute or two it needs to get all the release and change it wants to have at this point. Don't rush on. You just got here.

Fifth Movement: Asking

If a big shift, an opening, and a bodily release have already come during the earlier movements, you go right to the sixth movement, receiving what has come along with the shift.

For example, you might have gotten such a shift and change in the problem already, when you sat quietly with the felt sense, sensing its crux and its quality. Or it might have come along with a handle word or image. It might have come while you resonated the handle with the felt sense.

But more usually a well-fitting handle gives you a little tiny bit of a shift, just enough to know it is quite right. You feel its rightness several times over (resonating), until there has been all the bodily effect that this rightness can make. Now you need a shift, and there has not yet been one—at least not the kind that changes the problem.

Now comes the fifth movement, asking.

In this movement you ask the felt sense, directly, what it is. Usually this consists *of spending some time* (a minute or so, which seems very long) staying with the unclear felt sense, or returning to it again and again. The handle helps one do this.

You use the handle to help you to make the felt sense *vividly* present again and again. It isn't enough to remember how you just felt it moments ago. It needs to be right here, otherwise you can't ask it. If you lose hold of it, present the handle to yourself and ask, "Is this still here?" After a few seconds it is there again (as before, or slightly changed).

Now you can ask *it* what it is.

For example, if your handle was "jumpy," say "jumpy" to yourself till the felt sense is vividly back, then ask *it*: "What is it about this whole problem that makes me so jumpy?"

If you hear a lot of fast answers in your head, just let that go by and then ask again. What comes swiftly is old information from your mind. At first the question to the felt sense may not get down to it, but the second or third time you ask, it will. The felt sense itself will stir, in answer, and from this stirring an answer will emerge.

You can tell the difference between the merely mental answers and those from the felt sense. The mental answers come very fast, and they are rapid trains of thought. The mind rushes in and leaves no space for you to contact the felt sense directly. You can let all that go by, and then recontact the felt sense, using the handle again. When the felt sense is back, you ask *it*.

One of the most important procedures in focusing is this asking of "open questions." You ask a question, but then you deliberately refrain from trying to answer it through any conscious thinking process.

People usually think they know the answers to such questions, or they decide what the answer should be. They ask themselves closed questions—in effect, rhetorical questions that they themselves answer immediately. Don't do that to your felt sense. Asking a felt sense is very much like asking another person a question. You ask the question, and *then you wait*.

There is a distinct difference between forcing words or images *into* a feeling and letting them flow *out* of it. When you force them into it, you effectively smother it and prevent it from showing its real nature. You tell it, "Oh, I already know what *you* are. There's no sense wasting time on you."

The words and images that flow *out* of a feeling, by contrast, are the kind that make a freshly felt difference. They are the kind that make you say, "Hey! Hey, yeah, *that's* what it's all about!" These are the words and pictures that produce a body shift.

The body shift is mysterious in its effects. It always feels good, even when what has come to light may not make the problem look any better from a detached, rational point of view.

If the felt sense does not shift and answer right away, that is all right. Spend a minute or so with it. We do not control when a shift comes. (That is "grace.") What is crucial is the time you spend sensing it (returning again and again to it). If you spent time sensing something unclear that is right there, meaningful, about this problem, and you don't yet know what it is, then you are focusing.

Sometimes it helps to ask one of the following two questions; first try one, then later the other. With each you will need to make sure that the question reaches the felt sense. At first, usually, your mind will answer. Just repeat the question until the felt sense stirs.

1. "What is the worst of this?" (Or, "What is the 'jumpiest' thing about all this?" if your handle word was "jumpy.")
2. "What does the felt sense need?" (Or, "What would it take for this to feel OK?")

If you have contacted the felt sense in the usual asking, and then have also asked these two questions in turn, and spent a minute or so sensing the unclear felt sense each time, it may be good to stop focusing for the moment.

Focusing is not work. It is a friendly time within your body. Approach the problem freshly later, or tomorrow.

Sixth Movement: Receiving

Whatever comes in focusing, welcome it. Take the attitude that you are glad your body spoke to you, what*ever* it said. This is only one shift; it is not the last word. If you are willing to receive this message in a friendly way, there will be another. If you will go this step of change, which is next now, there will be more change, whatever is next later.

You need *not* believe, agree with, or do what the felt sense just now says. You need only receive it. You will soon deeply experience that once what comes with a shift is received, another shift will come. What your body then says will be quite different. So permit it to tell you now whatever it must say first.

For example, with a shift you may get something you need to do, that is, a need from deep inside you. But the first form in which it comes might be quite impossible for you. It might seem to require that you leave your spouse and children and job, and besides it might require much money. It is very important to protect this first form, in which your life-direction can be sensed, even though it does not now meet these realistic questions. Your body is changing, your life-direction is appearing, this is only one step. Let the questions wait. You aren't going to go right out to do something wild. Keep that new sense of what would be a right direction and don't worry now about the form it will eventually take.

Allow even a very little shift to have its full minute or so. "All right, now at least I know where the trouble is," you may find with a momentary relief. Then the critical questions want to wipe it out very quickly. "Yes, but what good is it if I can't get it to change?" "Is this real? Maybe I'm fooling myself." "What if I don't get another shift after this?" Protect the shift that just came from all these negative voices. They may be right, but they have to wait. Don't let them dump a truckload of cement on this new green shoot that just came up.

It is time enough later to find out for sure if this step on the problem is real. Right now give it a space in which to breathe. Let it develop. Sense it. Be with it.

You may want to stop focusing after this, or you may go on. But don't rush on immediately. In a minute perhaps you will.

If you decide to stop, sense that you really can leave this place and return to it later. It is very much like a *place*, a spot in your inner landscape. Once you know where it is and how to find it, you can leave it and come back tomorrow.

Whatever comes in focusing will never overwhelm you if you can have the attitude we call "receiving." You welcome anything that comes with a body shift, but you stay a little distance from it. You are not *in* it, but *next to* it. This space, in which you can be next to it, forms in a few moments, as your body eases. "I can't solve this all in one day," you say to yourself. "I know it's there. I can find it again. I can leave it for a while." You are neither running away nor going into it. You get a breath. You sense that there is space between it and you. You are here, it is there. You *have* it, you *are* not it.

Or you can imagine a door between it and you, if you wish one. You have your hand on the doorknob, and you can open it a little whenever you want.

Do You Want to Go Another Round of Focusing?

Sense if your body wants to stop focusing or to continue. Does it say, "Wait! I just got here, let me be here for a day or so. This feels new"? Or does it say, "Let's not stop here, this isn't a new place yet. I don't want to be left here!"? Imagine going on and sense its reaction, then imagine stopping and sense its reaction.

If you stop, then first take a minute to be sure you can get back the step you just got on your problem. Usually it isn't enough to remember the outcome. One remembers it later, but it may then lack the directly experienced realness it has now. It helps to recall what came just before the last shift. For example, suppose you had a "handle" image of a ball of wool tightly bound, and from asking what made that, your good shift came and moved your problem one step toward solution. You would remember not only that step itself but also what immediately preceded the shift. That helps, later on, when you recall the step, to get it back with full bodily realness. From the preceding image it will come back fully again. It helps to find this before stopping.

To go another round of focusing, you might freshly sense the whole problem, and ask your body, "Is it all solved?" The discomfort of what is still unresolved will then come definitely *in your body*, if you await it there. You would stay with this whole felt sense and go through the movements 2–6 as before.

Or you might go on from your last shift, from what came with it, by getting under *that*. "What now is the whole sense of *that?*"

As understanding and gentle and accepting as you were for that quiet minute, now you also want *further* change. By being gentle and understanding, by appreciating this feeling, you prepared the ground for that further change. To move into further change, you begin again with the second movement: get the felt sense that is *under* or beyond whatever body-message you just received.

Suppose, for example, that in the last round what emerged was that you feel "helpless," and you had a shift around, "Oh, that's what I've been feeling, and I'm so jumpy all the time from feeling that it will come to a crunch, and I'm really helpless!"

Now, to go another round, you ask yourself: "What is that whole felt sense, *all that* about helplessness?"

Ask—and don't answer. Let the feeling deepen itself. "Helpless" is still the right word, but it is now the word only for the tip of the iceberg. You can begin to feel its bulk beneath the word. All that—quite a lot—is involved in the whole bulk.

Again, the third movement: you try to sense the quality of this new, wider felt sense.

Whenever words come, you check them against the felt sense. If they make no difference there, you let them go by, and you return to the felt sense.

A felt shift feels like a release. That is how you recognize it. It may come at any time during any of the focusing movements. If that happens, welcome it. Also, some of the movements may happen simultaneously. These instructions deal not with a mechanical process but with a human one.

There may be many such cycles or steps before a given problem feels resolved. You feel a body shift with each step.

It often isn't possible to deal fully with a given problem in one focusing session. A dozen steps may be necessary, perhaps even a hundred, before the problem feels resolved. The process may take many months. You continue with each session until, simply, you feel you have had enough for the day. You reach a point where you say, "Well, I haven't beaten this problem yet, but I'm at a stopping place that feels pretty good. I need a day to let my body live with this much changed, and perhaps also to go out into the world and see what happens." Steps of focusing and steps of outward action often alternate. Each aids the other.

Don't get discouraged if focusing doesn't give you dramatic results the first time you try it. Like any other skill, it requires practice. Also, as we have seen, it requires you to overcome certain deeply ingrained habits of mind and body, certain too-familiar ways of talking to yourself and at yourself. To deal with such difficulties may take time.

My colleagues and I have taught focusing to many people over the past several years, and we have carefully noted the difficulties people regularly run into when exploring this unfamiliar internal territory. We know what to do about these difficulties. If you find that the experience of inner change eludes you at first—and the odds are, statistically, that you will—be assured that you aren't the first person to have encountered your particular problem. Whatever that problem is, we will probably be able to help with it before the book ends.

The remaining chapters of Part Two are designed for this purpose. They are troubleshooting chapters. They review the most common problems that interfere with people's focusing—they suggest ways to get unstuck.

The six movements:

1. **Clearing a space**
2. **The felt sense**
3. **Finding a handle**
4. **Resonating**
5. **Asking**
6. **Receiving**

Chapter 6
What Focusing Is Not

One very common difficulty experienced by new focusers is a confusion over what focusing is supposed to be. Most people absorb a layman's education in psychotherapy by the time they reach adulthood, and while this may be useful in some respects, it can also lead to faulty preconceptions.

If you start your focusing experience with any such error in your mind, you are very surely going to go off in a wrong direction. So:

Focusing Is Not a Process of Talking at Oneself

If you are like almost everybody else, you undoubtedly know a good deal about what is wrong in your life. You may often lecture yourself, perhaps basing your lectures on sound inferences and assumptions.

"It's my mother. She always hated men and said so all the time. I got that from her and I know better but I must still have some of that in me, or it wouldn't be so difficult for me to relate to men."

Or, at other times, you skip the sophisticated lecture and insult yourself roundly and simply instead. A kick is what you think you need.

"Oh sure, I know what my trouble is. No guts. No courage, that's me. No wonder I never get anywhere."

Not only do these lectures and self-castigations feel unpleasant, but they produce no useful change. You become something like two people, one in prison and the other outside. The outside person lectures or insults the one inside, cruelly listing all the alleged (but usually unproven) faults of character that have supposedly led to the prisoner's sorry plight None of this helps the prisoner escape. When the lecture is over, the inner person is, as always, stuck.

Focusing is not like that. Instead of talking at yourself from the outside in, you listen to what comes *from you*, inside. You ask in a quiet, friendly, and sympathetic way, "What's wrong?" You may never before have been quite this friendly to yourself. Most people treat themselves very badly, much worse than they would ever think of treating another human being. Most people deal with their inside feeling person as a sadistic prison guard would.

Now, having asked your body this question—"What's really wrong?"—you deliberately refrain from answering it. When you ask another person a question, you don't go right on and answer the question yourself. Treat your own inside feeling person at least as well as you would someone else. Your inside feeling person, too, can answer, and doesn't need you to do all the answering.

Try to pass up all the glib, familiar answers that come very fast. They are the same old answers you've heard in thousands of self-lectures down through the years. Firmly reject them. Wait quietly for fresh answers to come from the inside, from the bodily felt sense of whatever situation is troubling you.

Focusing Is Not an Analytic Process

It is fairly easy, even fun sometimes, to attempt a rational analysis of one's personal problems. Such an analysis can be elaborate or simple, very serious or a parlor game. Intellectuals can't help analyzing at least some of the time.

"The reason I'm alone *must* be because I pick the wrong men. I must be attracted to a type that eventually rejects me. It must be because I am looking for someone like my father."

Whether or not the basic assumptions behind this person's analysis are broadly correct, the analysis doesn't do her much good. Nothing inside her has changed. She is still stuck.

As a matter of fact, the very terms in which a self-analysis is conducted tend to emphasize that "stuck" quality. When you tell yourself, "That's the way I am," you imply that there is no possibility of change. Analysis is, in this sense, almost always pessimistic.

Focusing, by contrast, is optimistic. It is based on the very positive expectation of change. It doesn't envision a human being as a fixed structure whose shape can be analyzed once and for all. It envisions a person as a *process*, capable of continual change and forward movement. The "problems" inside you are only those parts of the process that have been stopped, and the aim of focusing is to unstop them and get the process moving again. When you are focusing correctly, you not only expect change; you create it in the very act of focusing.

Instead of trying to analyze a problem, you begin by getting in touch with the felt sense of it, *all* of it, the whole problem at once. It is a special kind of receptivity in which the felt sense can physically shift.

You can never conceptualize all the myriad details in "*all that* about the fight we had last night." But, having felt the problem whole, you can next get in touch with the crux, and then with what lies beneath that, and so on. You focus step by step, until the problem feels resolved.

Resolving a problem is very different from merely understanding it. In focusing, one doesn't merely talk about a problem. One *experiences* a physical shift in how it feels.

When focusing produces a real problem-solving step, the body shift signals that some inside stuckness has changed. With each step, the problem feels slightly different from and better than the way it felt before. The felt sense of it has changed—which is another way of saying *you* have changed. When you next meet the problem in a life situation, your reaction will be different.

A successful focusing step usually gives a much better, truer understanding of what has been wrong. Along with the physical felt shift, something comes in words or felt understanding, which explains the trouble much more clearly, and usually in new terms. Quite often, the whole difficulty is rooted in something different from any of the considerations you were looking at. And if you take *that* body-wisdom and then further focus on it, again something comes along with the next body shift. This may again surprise you and may not follow logically from what you got at the first step.

But sometimes one or more steps of this process of change can bypass your analytic mind completely. A change can happen without your understanding fully why or how it has happened. If you focus on that troublesome felt sense of "all about John," for example, you may find that the words that come along with the body shift add very little to your conscious understanding of your "John" problem. But understanding is a by-product.

Or what comes may seem beside the point. "So, all right," you might think, "now I know a new reason why I'm uncomfortable around John. Now I know there's something about my job tangled up in this, something about John thinking I don't try hard enough. But what good does it do me to know that? Next time I meet him, the problem will still be there, won't it?"

No. It won't, not if that came with a focusing body shift. The shift in focusing changed your felt sense of John in hundreds or maybe thousands of subtle ways that are beyond your power, or anybody's power, to perceive rationally. The changes have taken place in your body, not in your rational mind. Your conscious mind knows little about them. All you might ever know is that, next time you meet John, you will *feel* different and act different. (At times, one can *later* figure out some of it— if one wishes.)

The process is admittedly mysterious—not only to people who experience it for the first time but also to those of us who have studied it for years. We humans still know very little about our mind-and-body processes.

I can say with much more certainty *what* happens than *why*. I have seen it take place in many others and felt it take place in myself. Now let's make it happen in you.

Focus for the next ten minutes if you haven't done so already. Notice any difficulties you run into. The next chapters can help you with them.

Focusing Is Not a Mere
Body Sensation

A felt sense is the body's physical sense of a problem, or of some concern or situation. It is a physical sense of meaning. If you have bodily sensations that seem just purely bodily, and not related to any aspect of your life, let them go. Ask yourself how your life is going, and quite soon you will have a bodily felt sense.

Focusing Is Not Just Getting in Touch
with "Gut Feelings"

You might have a distinct and intense feeling in relation to some problem, and usually the same one over and over. Especially if you have had that feeling many times, there is little point in having it over again, one more time.

A felt sense is the broader, at first *unclear, unrecognizable* discomfort, which *the whole* problem (*all that*) makes in your body. To let it form, you have to stand back a little from the familiar emotion. The felt sense is wider, less intense, easier to have, and much more broadly inclusive. It is how your body carries *the whole* problem.

A quality-word as the handle of a felt sense is likely to be a word that doesn't yet say much about the problem. It would be a fitting word (or image) of your own. Words of that sort are "heavy," "tight," "like glue," "cowed," "jittery." Such words help one hold on to the quality of the as yet unclear felt sense.

Chapter 7
Clearing a Space for Yourself

The first movement of focusing is enormously important because if it can happen, the rest will probably happen too. In the first movement you clear a space for yourself to live in while the rest of the focusing process is going on.

Normally you will perform the first movement only once at the beginning of each focusing session. The other movements may be repeated dozens of times in a given session, as you go down through your felt senses in one step after another after another. Different people find different movements difficult at first. Don't be discouraged if the first one happens to be hard for you.

The first movement is the one in which you give yourself what might be called a "positive set." You put yourself into a state of mind and body in which the other focusing movements can take place freely. Your inner actions in this movement are much like the overt actions of artists when they start to work each morning. They make sure their brushes are cleaned and free of hardened paint, scrape dried residue off the palette, stir the pots and knead the tubes to work out any stiffening or coagulation that may have taken place in the paints overnight. This may seem to be peripheral to the main work, but until it is done, the rest of the work can't begin at all.

There are many ways to approach the first movement, many different inner acts that can produce the needed positive set—or body–mind receptivity. An approach that works well for one person might produce nothing for another. Keep the one or ones that have meaning for you personally, the approach or combination of approaches that make something good happen inside *you*.

Clearing a Cluttered Room

We've already looked at this room-clearing approach. It is the one that makes me call this first movement the act of "clearing a space." You push all your problems to one side so that there is a place for you to breathe and sit in temporary comfort. To use a slightly different example, this is like ...

Finding the Right Distance from Your Problems

You don't want to fall into your problems, sink in them, *become* them. Conversely, you don't want to run away from them, ignore them, or repress them. Those approaches are usually not fruitful.

There is a third way, a much more useful one. It is the inner act of *distancing* yourself from what is troubling you but still keeping it before you. You don't go into the problems. You stand back just a little way—far enough so that the problems no longer feel overwhelming, but close enough so that you can still feel them.

Stand a few feet back from your problems. You can walk up and touch them if you like, sense them there, as though with your fingertips. And you can pull back whenever they begin to get too threatening.

You do this with each of your problems in the first movement, one by one. You distance yourself from whatever is troubling you on that particular day, whatever is hurting you, nagging at you. You still see all those problems before you, of course. They are all still very much there. But you have stepped into a little sheltered space where, for a time, they cannot hurt you.

Permission to Feel Good

Some people have told me that this first movement somehow seems like escaping problems. They believe they must feel every bad feeling to the fullest at all times. If they don't, they are being cowardly. They seem to feel guilty about feeling good, even briefly. They feel it is their duty to feel bad incessantly as long as the problem is unsolved.

I tell them not to be concerned about feeling good for a little while. "You aren't escaping anything," I say. "Don't worry. While you feel good, you know that everything will stay just as bad as you know it is."

The mess will still be there and you will still have to clean it up. You aren't escaping it by taking a brief respite from it. As a matter of fact, you have done just the opposite. You have made yourself capable of handling it in a more effective and different way.

Not as a Monument

Think of the first movement as a brief time when you allow yourself to stop being a monument to your troubles.

Most people harbor a feeling that they must make their bodies express their troubles constantly. We live life with our bodies. Every trouble and bad situation is like a cramp in the body. As long as the body is cramped by trouble, it already has the shape of the trouble and therefore can't cope with that trouble as a fresh, whole body. It copes with the trouble while *being* the trouble. Therefore focusing begins with giving your body a pause, a break, in which to let it become whole.

Most people let their bodies be cramped into the shape of what's wrong with their lives, being a monument to all the things that are wrong, every moment.

But you *can* walk up to your poor body, standing there cramped, the monument to everything that's wrong, and say: "It's OK. We won't forget. You can rest a while. Later you can come back and stand as a monument again, but now, go take a break!"

The fear is of avoiding and forgetting. It is as if you had only two choices: either avoid or feel terrible. But there is a third choice: let the body feel whole and sound, don't become the embodiment of your troubles, just have them in front of you. You have not avoided them and yet you are not totally overwhelmed by them.

If you can do that just for a minute, you will be ready to work on the difficulties and painful feelings in a new way.

Setting Down the Burden

To use another analogy, your inner act in the first movement of focusing is like the act of putting down a heavy burden you have been carrying. You have walked for miles with this uncomfortable bag. Now you stop, set it down, and rest for a while. Only by first setting it down can you look at what's in the bag.

Your body needs the rest. You load it with this burden every morning and, if you are like most people, give it no rest until you go to sleep. Perhaps there is a brief time when you awake on some mornings when your body is allowed to feel good. You must have had the experience. Your eyes open. You feel gloriously relaxed and peaceful.

And then the load lands on you! You remember all the problems that were troubling you yesterday. Each morning we load ourselves with this heavy paraphernalia and stagger through the day with it. In the first movement of focusing, you unload. Put the heavy pack down on the ground. Take the problems out one by one and line them up and look at them without carrying them.

The Comforting List

Still another way to think about the first movement: it is like making a "things-to-do" list.

Undoubtedly you have experienced the tension of having too many things to do and too little time in which to do them. A kind of panic may arise before you go away on vacation, for example, or on a long trip. In the few days before you take off, you find yourself running around in circles.

In that state you are very likely to do that which you dread: forget something important. How can you calm yourself? By sitting down and making a list of what needs to be done.

Making the list doesn't get the jobs done, of course.

What it does do is to make you feel better. It alleviates the panic, puts you into a state in which you can approach the central problem in a calm, orderly way.

Body Trust

In seeking this first-movement state of tranquillity, you will find it helps to trust in your body.

Let your body return to its natural state—which is perfect. The body can feel completely at ease and natural every moment. Just let it.

Once your body is allowed to be itself, uncramped, it has the wisdom to deal with your problems. You will be dealing with these tense feelings and situations with a relaxed, loose body.

It is true that this little bit of good feeling—this rest you are giving your body by stacking the troubles in front of you—is incomplete.

But also expect, soon, when you start to work on this stack, that you will feel much better. Your body always tends in the direction of feeling better. Your body is a complex, life-maintaining system.

Often, we feel so much wrong that we come to accept those bad feelings as the basic state of things. But it is not. The bad feeling is the body knowing and pushing toward what good would be.

Every bad feeling is potential energy toward a more right way of being if you give it space to move toward its rightness.

The very existence of bad feelings within you is evidence that your body knows what is wrong and what is right. It must know what it would be like to feel perfect, or it could not evoke a sense of *wrong*.

Your body, with its sense of rightness, knows what would feel right. The feelings of "bad" or "wrong" inside you are, in effect, your body's measurement of the distance between "perfect" and the way it actually feels. It knows the direction. It knows this just as surely as you know which way to move a crooked picture. If the crookedness is pronounced enough for you to notice it at all, there is absolutely no chance that you will move the picture in the wrong direction and make it still more crooked while mistaking that for straight. The sense of what is wrong carries with it, inseparably, a sense of the direction toward what is right.

The moral and ethical values we *think about* and try to control may be relative and various, but the values by which our bodies move away from bad feelings are much more objective. Of course, the body also learns more as we develop. It does not sense every possible value already. But it senses vastly more than we can think. The body is an incredibly fine system within nature and the cosmos. Its *holistic* sensing of what is prolife and what is not indicates much more than a thought or an emotion can. If we wish to add something, we must sense how that can fit into what the body senses already—its own values. We may not be able to *say* what these values are, without contradicting ourselves or making ungrounded assumptions, but the life process in us has its direction and this is not relative. All the values we try to formulate are relative to the living process in us and should be measured against it.

In focusing you will often find that some words, which

come with a strong sense of rightness at a given moment and give you a body shift, are later superseded by what comes at a later step. You cannot—and should not—trust any *single* set of words, any *one* feeling, any *one* body-message that comes. But you can definitely trust the whole series of steps by which your body moves to resolve and change a wrong state of being. You can trust that, even if the words and understanding of a given step are superseded, that step was the right step to come then, at that moment, and will lead to the right next step from there.

When I use the word "body," I mean much more than the physical machine. Not only do you physically live the circumstances around you, but also those you only *think* of in your mind. Your physically felt body is in fact part of a gigantic system of here and other places, now and other times, you and other people—in fact, the whole universe. This sense of being bodily alive in a vast system is the body as it is felt from inside.

When something goes wrong, the body knows it and immediately sets about the task of repairing itself. The body knows what its own right state feels like and is constantly checking and adjusting its processes to stay as close to that state as possible. It maintains its temperature, for instance, in a narrow range near 98.5 degrees. People all over the world have precisely the same body temperature, whether they live on the Equator or in the Arctic. Your temperature stays in the same range through summer and winter, in exercise or repose, for your body knows what *right* is and continually monitors and adjusts and compensates to maintain the proper balance.

You don't have to exercise any conscious control over

this temperature-maintaining process. You trust your body to carry the process on day by day—and you also trust it to know when something is going wrong. It always does know. When your temperature slips out of that narrow "right" range, you feel unmistakably less than good.

Medical help only ministers to the body, only helps here and there with what is always the body's own healing process. A doctor knows how to help heal a wound, but the wound heals itself. Similarly, whatever you do, sense then whether it has helped your body's healing take a step or not.

Your body knows the direction of healing and life. If you take the time to listen to it through focusing, it will give you the steps in the right direction.

A Vast Space

The first movement (clearing a space) can be done alone, for its own sake. If you do it very slowly, you may come to a state that seems important in its own right. Then you might leave the rest of focusing for another time.

To do the first movement in this way is more elaborate. You put your attention in your body, and you propose to your body that you feel totally fine and joyful *about how your life is going*. Then you sense what comes there, usually some discomfort about something in your life. You see what that is (large or trivial doesn't matter), and you acknowledge it ("Yes, that's there"). Then you place it next to yourself, in a friendly way, as if on the floor.

Now you ask your body, "What would come, *in my body*, if this problem were somehow all solved?" Whatever your mind answers, you wait until you sense what comes in your body. Then you let that be for a little while.

Now you ask, "Except for this, do I feel totally fine and joyful about how my life is going?" You do the same thing with what next comes. Each time, you wait for the way your body responds to the questions.

After the five or six things that usually come in this way, there is one more: There is usually, for each person, a "background feeling" that is always there (for instance, "always gray," "always a little sad," "always running scared," "always trying hard"). What quality is always there, now too, and comes between you and feeling fine? Set it aside as well ("Sometime I'll see what more goes with that...not now"). Again ask, "What would come in my body, if that were also set aside?"

By this means you can sometimes come to an opening out, a sense of a vast space.

Under all the packages each of us carries, a different self can be discovered. *You are* not any of the things you have set aside. You are no content at all!

When you arrive at this wide space, you might want to stay a while and just be there. But to arrive there involved specific questions put to your body, and a wait for some specific response from your body.

The Friendly Hearing

The first movement is the time when you establish an environment of friendly feeling within yourself. You prepare to give yourself a fair hearing.

"How are you now?" you ask, gently. "What's with you right now? What's the main thing for you right now?"

And then you don't answer in words. No, you wait. Let the answer be the feelings that will come in your body.

People can always think of some long list of things that might, or ought to, trouble them. This is not the list we want. We want only to hear what is now keeping your body from feeling sound.

At first you might hit a blank and become impatient, because after all, you think you know. "I'm fine, except for my bad feeling, as usual, about my main relationship, and that other worry." But this is answering your question yourself. The body doesn't answer that quickly. It takes about thirty seconds.

Surely you would be willing to accord your body thirty seconds? And yet, oddly, most people *never* do.

Look at your watch and see how long thirty seconds is. This will make you aware of their surprisingly lengthy span. Take thirty seconds. Try it now.

We've noted before that most people are pretty unfriendly toward themselves most of the time. If you are like most, you have treated yourself less like a friend than like a roommate you don't like. You grumble at yourself, insult yourself, get impatient with yourself when things go wrong. You construct a model of the ideal person you wish you were, and then you condemn yourself because you are imperfect as measured against that ideal. "Oh, I'm just lazy," you insult yourself. "If I really wanted to get somewhere I'd work harder. I set up these good goals for myself and then I back off and flounder and make excuses."

And so the lecture goes. Until you have focused, you

haven't sat down and asked in a quiet and friendly way what is really there. "Lazy" is only an external word, an insult. The word "lazy" says only that nothing important could be involved in how you do feel. But your body knows why and how you are as you are, and some of that will turn out to be important if you will give it a friendly hearing.

Society mostly gives you the same unfriendly hearing you probably give yourself. "Shape up," the world says. Results are wanted of course, but sometimes they are wanted so quickly, so tensely that there's not a minute to see what is in the way. Yet one minute can make a vast difference. Other people often don't want to know what is really stopping us or frustrating us. "Just do it right." The inward complexity, which can stop us but can also make us better, more effective, interesting, and creative, is often not welcome. There are those condemning words— "lazy," "not motivated," "selfish," "self-pitying," "too sensitive," "too demanding"—which do not really describe what is in us, but rather, dismiss what is in us. But we must look inside ourselves.

Suppose you are interviewing a rather shy person who hasn't been allowed to say much for some time, perhaps some years. You would not get impatient and yell at the person after five seconds. You would ask questions gently and then wait at least thirty seconds before concluding that the person was a hopeless idiot and also empty and incapable of speech. Nor would you reject the first thing that was said.

This doesn't mean I am demanding that you change yourself completely before you even begin focusing. I am not suggesting that you can be self-accepting and self-loving and all the things you'd like to be and perhaps are not just by reading these pages. Rather, it is an attitude you can take for this special time of focusing.

There is also some strong, harsh voice that interrupts loudly when one tries to listen inwardly. Sometimes it is a critical part of oneself. Sometimes, however, it is a perfectly good life energy that is impatient. "I've been in the same spot for years, now I want something to get me out." This is a perfectly justified feeling, but it too must wait. "But I've waited all my life." Sure, but now wait only these few minutes so we can hear from your internal self. Let's ask gently, "What do you feel down in there?"

It is important in the first focusing movement to establish this atmosphere of a friendly hearing. Be prepared to accept for a moment whatever feelings you find inside. Don't argue with them.

An unfriendly hearing is one in which certain answers or all answers are rejected before they are even fully heard. It is the kind of hearing an angry teacher gives a disruptive child. It is the kind you have probably given yourself too often:

"Well, what do you have to say for yourself? How do you explain this new mess you've gotten us into?"

"Well, I—"

"Shut up! I'll tell you what your trouble is...."

The first movement of focusing is not like that. In this movement you smile at yourself, hold out your hand to yourself. "Hello, there," you say. "How are you feeling now?" Having asked that question, you carefully avoid answering it. Let the answer come from inside, and accept it for the moment. "Lots of problems." "Oh, lots of problems huh? Well, OK, let's just clear a space among them for a while, so we can sit in peace.... Which problem feels the heaviest right now? That one?... Ah, that sex business, is it? What else?"

Keep your cleared space. When you begin to focus, don't be inside any of these things. Stand back, or stand next to, what you focus on. Ask: "How does that feel today, *all that* about sex?"

And you are into the second movement with every chance of making something shift.

Chapter 8
If You Can't Find a Felt Sense

In the preceding chapter we looked at various ways of successfully making the first focusing movement happen. Now in much the same way, we will look at ways of overcoming possible problems you may encounter in the second movement. This, you recall, is the movement I call "feeling for the whole of the problem"—the one in which you let form an overall felt sense of a problem or situation that is troubling you, the sense of *all that*.

As before, I will offer several suggestions for overcoming diverse difficulties. Look upon this chapter, like the last, as a selection of tools put at your disposal. Take those that seem useful.

Where to Look for a Felt Sense

You may have had trouble making contact with your felt sense of a problem or you may not have been sure you can recognize a felt sense as such when it comes. There are no ready-made words in the language for it and so it is hard to describe. Until now very few people understood it. Society, and thus also language, viewed only the resulting manifestations—thoughts, emotions, perceptions—not the felt sense. Even psychotherapists knew of it only as a mysterious something. Only our recent research makes it discussable and teachable.

So let me talk a little more about what a felt sense is.

A felt sense is made of many interwoven strands, like a carpet. But it is felt (or "seen," if we pursue the carpet analogy) *as one.*

A felt sense is the many-stranded fabric of bodily awareness that (for example) guides golfers as they tee off. It would be impossible for them to *think* all the details of location, surrounding environment, and body movement that are woven into aiming. But the body knows the complex set of coordinated movements it must make to swing. The single felt sense of the situation incorporates the problem and the bodily known solution.

Golfers cannot think out all these details intellectually. When a golfer swings, several hundred different muscles must all work together in a precise way, each coming into action at a certain microsecond, each exerting just the right amount of pull on the right bone for the right length of time. The body feels all this as a whole.

If you observe a golfer getting ready to swing, you can see the whole body taking aim. It's done not just with the eyes or the arms but by changing the placement of the feet, rotating and repositioning the whole body. Golfers aim with the feel of the whole body.

It may be that conscious direction is needed on one part of the process. The golfer may be thinking, "This time I must keep that left elbow straighter." But all the other aim-taking motions occur without conscious thought as the golfer thinks about that left elbow. The preliminary movements are guided by the whole body's feel, finding its balance, seeking the feeling that says, "Yes, now I am ready, I feel right. Now I can swing." Golfers cannot describe that feeling of "ready," because too many details are involved. They know the feeling when it comes, however. When the body-feel is right, they swing.

You look for a felt sense in the same place where golfers look to find whether they are ready to swing. They don't ask the question in their heads, they feel for the answer in their bodies.

The same process of feeling within the body is familiar in any other sport. Asking questions in the head, or trying to make the head dominate the body, never works.

There is another way to get at this question of where and how to look for a felt sense—another kind of example that may be more familiar and useful to you. Suppose you have been listening to a discussion and are about to say something relevant and important. The others are still talking. You don't have your words prepared. All you have is a felt sense of what you want to say.

Only rarely, in very formal occasions, do we prepare word for word. Usually, when we are about to say something, we have *the felt sense* of what we want to put across, and the right words come as we speak. The felt sense includes dozens of component parts, perhaps hundreds: the meaning you want to put across, the emotional color you want to give it, the reasons why you want to say it to those particular people, the reaction you hope to elicit from them, and so on. But there are not yet any specific words.

Now suppose that, as you wait for your chance to speak, your attention is distracted for a moment and you lose hold of what you were about to say. The others are now giving you your turn, waiting for you to say what you wanted to say, but you cannot.

You never did have words to say, so you can't use words as a memory hook to fish up your lost meaning. What do you do to regain the sense of what you were going to say? Where do you look for it?

You look within the body. You go through a process that is much like an informal kind of focusing; you grope inside yourself. There you do have a felt sense—but not the ready-to-speak open felt sense you had before. Instead, you have that *feeling* of what you forgot.

You might try simply becoming quiet, receptive, hoping that "it" will open and what it was will come flooding back by itself. Or you can ask yourself questions: "Was it something about...?" Or you can try to trace logical connections: "They were talking about such-and-such, so it must have had to do with..." Or you can try to re-create the lost meaning by surrounding it with events like a lost piece of jigsaw puzzle: "It came to me right after Carol said... and then, before I opened my mouth, Lou said..."

Any of these processes might help lead you to "it," but "it" must respond. When it does, when it opens and what you wanted to say comes back, the physically felt release tells you that you've got it. And even at that moment, when you again "know" what you wanted to put across to those other people, you still don't have it in words.

Both when you knew what you wanted to say, and when you knew only that you had forgotten it, there was a felt sense. One can even say that it is "the same" felt sense—but when it returns, the felt sense opens and lets you discover and use what it was.

Focusing is very much like that. One must go to that place where there are not words but only *feeling. At first there may be nothing there until a felt sense forms.* Then when it forms, it feels pregnant. The felt sense has in it a meaning you can feel, but usually it is not immediately open. Usually you will have to stay with a felt sense for some seconds until it opens. The forming, and then the opening of a felt sense, usually takes about thirty seconds, and it may take you three or four minutes, counting distractions, to give it the thirty seconds of attention it needs.

When you look for a felt sense, you look in the place you know without words, in body-sensing.

Practice in Getting a Felt Sense

1. Silently, to yourself, pick something you love or think is beautiful. It could be an object, a pet, a place, or whatever. Something very special to you in some way. Take from one to two minutes.
2. Settle on one thing. Ask yourself "Why do I love _____, or why do I think it's beautiful?"
3. Let yourself feel that whole sense of specialness or loving. See if you can find one or two words that get at what it is.
4. Let yourself feel what those words *refer to*, to the whole felt sense, and see if new words and feelings come up.

This exercise is to help you get experience attending to a felt sense, something large and definitely felt, but that you are not able to verbalize. Notice how little of your love-feeling the words actually say. Yet the words are somehow right in relation to the felt sense (if you succeeded in finding such words).

One Way to Let a Felt Sense Form

Remember my description, earlier, of how we try to tell ourselves we feel fine, and yet in the body the bad feeling talks back? We say, "It's fine, it's all OK! That doesn't bother me at all," and yet, if we check the body, what comes there feels just as bad as before.

This can be used to help get a felt sense.

Suppose you are focusing on a problem. You *know*, of course, that you don't feel fine about it, since it is a problem for you. Even so, try proposing *to your body*, "I feel all fine about this, the problem is all solved." If you put your attention in your body, you will quite quickly find that a very specific not-fine sense about the problem comes there.

Of course, you knew all along that you didn't feel fine about the problem, but now you can sense the exact quality of the felt sense, how your body has the problem.

The same method can also be used at any time, during focusing, if you lose hold of the felt sense and feel lost. You just put your attention in your body, and you say, "So, this problem is now all solved ... right?" Wait a moment—and there is your body-sense of what is still unresolved. Then sense the quality of that.

A Mural of the Whole Problem

Sometimes it helps to begin with an image and then find the felt sense. Imagine that your *whole* problem is a very large picture on a wide wall. You have to step back to see it all. Let such an image come, then attend in your body for what felt sense that image gives you.

When Words Get in the Way

If you have been living with a problem for a good deal of time, you have probably formed words to describe or explain the problem and you are probably stuck on those words. This happens to most people. "I *know* what my problem about sex is," someone might say. "I'm scared of it. Just scared. I can feel it. What else is there to say?"

Obviously nothing will shift if those words are always in the way. They are pessimistic words, denying the possibility of change. "This is the way I am," the words say. "I was built this way, or my life has made me this way. I'm stuck here."

We've talked before about the trick of letting such words go by, ignoring what we know and sensing freshly to find what your body really feels. Take the feeling you have and let it broaden out into the felt sense of all that.

Another way to get this is to say to yourself, "What does it now feel like to me, to be a person who has this problem?" Immediately, you will feel something wider, which at first isn't clear. Focus on that. Or it may be immediately clear what the feeling quality of it is. It may be anger at having the problem, or urgency to solve it, or a heavy hopeless feeling, or perhaps some sense of being small and tense. To ask what it feels like, now, to be a person with this problem, helps widen the scope, so that the felt sense of the whole problem can come and then give you other specific feelings. Then focus on the main feeling quality of what comes.

Another specific aid: If words keep coming into your head, explanations and ideas and accusations and so on, keep repeating an open-ended question of your own. For example, keep repeating, "What does this *whole* thing feel like?" That way you control the word-making part of your mind yourself, so it can't run off with you.

But the point isn't to fight words. It is quite all right for words to flow. The point is to feel behind and beyond them. To do this, it helps to keep repeating an open-ended question.

It is important not to stay stuck with the same old thoughts and feelings, but to widen the scope so that a different process can begin from the body's wider sense of the trouble.

When There Is No Feeling Apart from the Words

If you haven't been able to experience any feeling or felt sense that is clearly different from words, if your feeling always comes along with words that fit the feeling perfectly, so that they are always all one, try this:

Go through the first focusing movements as usual: clear a space, stack all your troubles to one side, sit quietly and receptively. Then repeat the most feeling-filled words you have, slowly, a dozen times or so: "I'm scared of it. . . . scared of it. . . ." And all the time, keep some questions hovering around the words: "What is this 'scared'? What does it feel like, inside? Where do I feel it?"

At first the words and feeling may be exactly all one,

but after a while you will find the feeling growing somewhat larger, sticking out around the edges of the words, so to speak. You will find that, yes, the words are right but they get only the center of the feeling. Actually there is more to the feeling.

As one of our best focusing teachers in Chicago told me:

"At first, when I tried to focus, I could never get a felt sense. All I had were words that I could feel, but there never was any feeling except right in the words. My words were like definitions and I had my feelings defined so they seemed as if they were exactly the same as the words. I was only looking at the center of each feeling, and in the center the feeling *was* what the words said. It took me three months till one day I noticed that there was more to the feeling. It had, sort of, fuzzy edges. They were beyond what the words got. That was the breakthrough for me. The feeling as having fuzzy edges, that's the felt sense. I teach it that way now."

To find the fuzzier edge of the feeling, or to get the feeling separate from the words, it can help to repeat the most meaningful phrase or sentence you can find, trying to sense where and what it makes you feel.

In a way, you are now going through the focusing movements backward. This works well for some people. The most common procedure is to make contact first with the felt sense of the problem as a whole (second movement). But as I have said before, focusing is not a mechanical procedure. If you find that it is more effective for you sometimes to start with words and work backward to the felt sense of *all that*, by all means do it that way.

But if you do, be sure that your inner attitude is one of *asking*, not telling. It won't do any good simply to repeat what you have been telling yourself for years. Repeat the words, yes, but in the spirit of *asking* how your body experiences them, and let your body-feeling answer.

Relaxing Your Body

It may help to stretch and relax all the parts of your body for a few minutes, before you begin focusing. Tense your arms, hands, forearms; let them feel tight, hard, tense. Feel the tension ... slowly relax. Feel the difference. Let them feel loose, soft, relaxed. Do that with your legs, stomach, jaw, all over. Check to see if you are "holding on" anywhere, and let yourself relax.

When Nothing Feels Bodily

"Before I could learn to focus," someone said to me, "I had first to discover how the ordinary emotions were really *in* my body. I used to feel fear and anxiety and excitement, of course, but I used to feel them all around me. Like they were in the air, sort of. It took me some time to realize that they were *in my body*, like my heart pounding, or a sinking feeling in my gut. I had to learn this first about the ordinary things everybody feels, that they were inside. Only then could I look for a felt sense inside."

If this report fits you, give yourself a week or so in

which to catch yourself whenever you feel any ordinary emotion strongly. Notice what your body feels like. You will find that your body feels the emotion *inside*.

Test yourself now. Can you put your attention inside your stomach? If you can, you sense a distinct feeling there, perhaps warm and fuzzy, perhaps tight and tense. If you cannot get such a sensation in your stomach, then you need to work on this. Put your attention in your left big toe; wiggle it if necessary. Press it down. Now you feel the sensation in it. Now come up to your knee. This time don't move your knee, just see if you can find it from inside. Then move to your groin, and from there move up into your stomach. There you are.

This is quite new to many people, but it does not take long to learn. Most people can put their attention in their stomach or chest, and if you work at it a little, so can you.

If You Find Your Mind Wandering

If you find yourself drifting off on some irrelevant train of thought when focusing, bring yourself back *gently*. Say: "What was I focusing on? . . . Oh, yeah, *that*. . . . And what was I trying to do with it? Oh, yeah, feel the whole thing. What does that whole thing feel like?"

To bring yourself back, you need to be gentle, something like dealing with a small child, whose attention is wandering. You put your arms around the child to attract its attention, and you gently guide it to whatever lesson you want to teach.

So when your mind wanders, gently put your arm around yourself, so to speak, and guide yourself back. It doesn't matter how many times you have to do that.

If You Have Few Feelings

Some people find it difficult to make contact with their feelings. Nearly everybody has this difficulty at least sometimes. A friend might show you a favorite painting, for example. You look at the painting, aware that the friend expects a meaningful comment from you. But the painting arouses no response in you—or, if it does, you can't quite get in touch with those feelings. You stare at the painting and finally you have to say, "Well, it's—uh—nice."

It may seem to you that you are simply not very complicated inside, that you don't have that complexity of feeling strands that I am describing in this book. But you do have it. You are human. It is there.

We are so accustomed to the simple patterns—if someone cheats us we are mad, if someone ignores us we are hurt—that many people don't look beneath these simple patterns to their own unique complexity. But it is there. When at first I might ask how you feel about being ignored, you might say, "Bad...how would *you* feel?" This would indicate that all people would feel "bad" or "hurt" when they are ignored, and indeed that is true. But just how and where it gets me is not the same as just how and where it gets you. This "just how and where" is beneath the simple feeling that is patterned and universal. To make touch with that could take a little time.

You have to say to yourself, "Yes...that's right...I feel hurt, and that's natural, yes, of course I know why. They ignored me. Sure, that's it, *but*...let me sense *all that* which is involved for me in this. It has to do with all-about-that person and all-about-me-with-that person, and all-about-what-it-means-to-me-to-get-ignored-anyway." Soon you will feel that mass of things not yet clearly known. Then you can focus on that felt sense and then on its crux.

If you find it hard to get in touch with your more complex feelings, there are several things you can do. It may be just a question of practice. Some people check their own feelings regularly, day by day, hour by hour, but perhaps you have never done this. Try it for the next few days. Identify feelings as they go by. As you interact with others and go through your daily life, stop inwardly once in a while and ask in a friendly way, "How am I now? What am I feeling now?" Don't tell yourself the answer. Wait. See what comes.

It feels good to do this, as long as you receive what you find inside. Don't say bad things to yourself and insult yourself over what you find. Just be pleased that you have found it, that it is clearly felt. Come to know your inside space.

If someone is often with you, it may help you make contact with your feelings if you ask that person to tell you when you clearly display a specific feeling. "You look angry," the person might say. Or, "I can see you're happy now." Other people will often be right in guessing that you have a feeling—though they are not likely to be right in guessing what that feeling really is. When your friend says you have a feeling look, be grateful, but don't take the friend's word as to what the feeling might be. Check inside. Your friend's assessment, "You look angry," may be quite wrong. You may find, instead, that you feel upset, worried, annoyed, impatient, disappointed, apprehensive, or perhaps some odd way that has no name. Go further into sensing what is in it.

If it has no name, that may be the best result of all. When you casually apply one of those well-worn unit-labels to a feeling—angry, scared, bored—the tendency is to think you now know everything there is to know about that feeling. You have given it its unit-label, you have identified it, and that's that. But there is always much, much more to know, for there is an infinity of possible ways to feel any labeled feeling such as anger. My "angry" right now sticks up from a different mass of things from another "angry" I will feel in a different situation tomorrow or next week. That is why you need not stop with feelings that seem to come with ready-made labels. Welcome especially those that come without names. When a feeling has no name, pause, listen, and let fresh words flow from it: "I feel... like I ought to be able to do something about this, but... I'm walled in, or something."

If You Feel Blank, or Stuck, or Empty

For focusing, just about anything will turn out to be a feeling. The absence of feeling is also a feeling, as I've said before.

"I am empty." "OK. What does this 'empty' feel like? What is the feel of all of this empty?"

"I'm stuck." "OK, what does this 'stuckness' feel like?" Find out if it is a tense stuckness, or heavy, like a boulder lying on top of you, or a not-knowing-what-to-do sort of stuckness. Or does it feel trapped? Give it time, and it will open up.

If You Are Angry at Yourself, or Trying Too Hard, or Too Restless or Afraid to Focus

Whatever gets in the way, you can focus on that for the moment, instead of the problem or difficulty you wanted to focus on. It may be that your body needs this obstacle to be removed first.

The obstacle is anger, let's say. Ask yourself, "OK, what is all-about-this-anger?" Let that feeling broaden out into its felt sense.

Or:

"There I go again, trying so hard I get all tense. OK, what is this trying so hard? I know all about it, of course, it's...yes, wait, I know all that. Let's just feel what is *all that* about trying so hard. All that. What does all that feel like?"

Or:

"I feel too restless to focus. I'm too jumpy. I wish I weren't so jumpy, so I could let my attention down inside. OK, let's take the jumpy. What is the whole feel of this jumpy?"

In this way you respect your body's sense of what has to be taken up next. Usually that turns out to be a new and better way into the problem.

When You Are Afraid to Focus

"I don't want to look inside myself. I'm scared of what I might find down there."

This is a common worry. But in focusing, you can treat yourself gently. Take yourself by the hand and say, "It's all right, we will not force you to go where you don't want to go. If you're afraid of that place, we'll keep our distance. We'll stay right here and see what the fear is. All right? What does this 'fear' feel like from here?..."

Or you might say to yourself, "I feel scared to focus on that. Probably something unpleasant in there I don't want to look at. All right...wait...if I don't want to go into it I am not going to. But I won't back off either. I'll just stay right here, where I don't want to focus, and I'll see: what is this feeling of not wanting to? Scared. OK, let's just stay right here, with this 'scared.' What is this 'scared'? What kind of 'scared' is it? What is the whole feel of it?"

The procedure of focusing feels good. The moment it doesn't, back up a little bit and see what it is that doesn't feel good.

Don't push yourself across barriers. Instead, focus on the immediate felt barrier. What is the whole feel of *that*?

There may be bad or scary feelings to focus on, but the focusing itself always feels good and makes the feeling less bad or scary. When it opens, your body releases and again that feels better. Your guide in focusing is toward these ways of feeling better, localizing and opening, releasing, fresh air. You will feel better, whatever you find down inside yourself, when you let it name itself and be localized.

If You Avoid Your Feelings

Some people, including psychologists, think that there are scary things inside themselves. This is fallacious.

Nameless horrors and weird states are not lying there "inside" you, like poisonous snakes locked in a cage. Many people talk of themselves this way. "I don't want to open the lid," they say. "I don't want to let all that bad stuff come out."

The truth is that you are not a cage full of snakes. You are not any kind of container in which feelings writhe around with lives of their own. You are a process, and your feelings are a part of that process.

For example, there is the way I felt with my father when he wouldn't listen to me, a feeling of helpless anger. Isn't that the same feeling I had then, have now, and can have whenever I bring it back to myself? Yes, but I am never *just* this feeling. I am a whole body. Therefore this feeling that I call "helpless anger" comes along with a thousand other things. Each time this feeling comes back to me it has a different totality with it.

When, in focusing, I ask my body to let me have more of what's in that whole feeling, the very way I approach myself changes the totality. The good-feeling focusing process itself changes much of the surroundings in which this feeling is now produced. My memory of my boyhood feeling won't change, but the way my whole body produces the feeling will be different. And that is one way to understand why focusing allows the body to change what has long been stuck and unchanging in us.

This means that we need not be scared of what is in

us—for there are no things in us. Rather, our feelings are newly produced each moment.

If Too Many Feelings Come Too Fast

Some people find focusing difficult because their feelings come too fast and there are too many. Focusing is a *slowing down* for these people. "Take any one, and stop it, and stay with it," I tell them.

Sometimes it helps when I say, "All right, there's that whole welter of feelings, now let it all be, and just let yourself quietly down under it, as if there is just one feeling under them all. See if you can get that feeling under them all." (Silence . . . then . . . "Oh, yes, I feel (say) hurt.") "OK, there you are," I say. "See what that hurt really is, that whole sense of hurt."

"Take charge," I say. "Throw them all out, and then let them come in one at a time. First, get them all off of you. Just sit up, look around the room, and push them all off. Take a break. Then let one feeling come—just one."

If Your Critic Makes You Feel Bad

Everyone has a "critic," a nasty voice that comes and says something like "Anything you do won't work," or "You're no good. You're worthless, nobody would want you around" or "You messed up again, you always do. This is another one in that long string" or "You're just a wishy-washy, no courage, that's you."

Sometimes this voice will use true information, but even so, its tone of voice is so nasty, you can tell it is the destructive critic attacking you.

It is very important to sense that the critic is different from your own inward source. The critic is *not* your own felt sense speaking from within you. Rather, it is like a voice coming at you from outside, or above your head. It waves its finger at you, like an angry parent or a mean teacher.

Naturally it generates feelings in you, but these are not feelings to focus on. They are only constrictions and tight-closed tensions the critic makes in you. *Do not respect your critic*. The critic is not your conscience. Conscience is a "still small voice" inside. You can evaluate any information much better yourself, if you first send the critic out into the hall, to wait. Your own sense comes from within you and always feels like an opening, an *un*-constricting. You may find the same facts, or you may not. Either way it is an entirely different kind of body-experience to focus.

The best way to deal with the critic (everyone has one!) is to wave it away with some disrespectful comment. Mine usually says the same things, over and over. So I say to it, "Go away and come back when you have something new to say."

Or I say, "I don't have to listen to anybody who talks to me in that tone."

All psychologists have found this destructive part of every person and given it various names (super-ego, bad parent, animus, critic). Whatever you call it, don't fall for it. In focusing one must push it out of the way when it interrupts. Wave it off with your hand, and put your attention in your body. Let the constriction the critic has made there ebb away. Wait till you are again sensing your own inward source, where the felt sense of the whole problem forms.

One person put it quite well: "It used to give me a thud, a thump in the middle. It was a signal to feel terrible. Now it's a signal to get mad. It's like somebody kicked me. 'You stop that!' " (She puts her fists up.)

Don't just believe your critic and focus on how bad it makes you feel. Instead, find out, underneath, what *you* really feel and perceive, and need. Work down where *you* feel and need things, and not just with your critic.

"I Go Right to My Bad Feeling, and Feel Bad as Always"

Some people, despite the careful and precise focusing instructions, skip them all and go directly to their usual bad feelings. Some people are used to turning to a single bad feeling inside, whenever they turn inside. So they begin to focus and there it is.

After I give focusing instructions in a group, I often ask each person to write me a note about whatever difficulty was encountered in trying to focus. One woman wrote: "When I came in here I felt fine, I focused on my bad feeling, and now I feel bad. Is this what focusing is for?"

Clearly, if that's focusing, who needs it? This is not focusing. Focusing involves letting a felt sense form something wider than and different from your old familiar bad feeling. Stay out of the old familiar sinkhole, stand back and take in a wider sense of the whole problem area that the bad feeling is part of.

For example, don't just remember your hurt at the

love relationships that just broke up. Instead, stand back and ask for a felt sense to form—a sense of the whole area: you and loving. Yes, yes, there's the hurt, but what else is there? What is the whole feel around and under it?

Sure, you know your particular depressed place. There might even be a suction drawing you into it, but don't sink. Ask yourself what that whole area of your life feels like, and you will find yourself out of the emotion, and a felt sense *under* it will come.

Strange as it sounds, focusing is *lighter* than heavy emotions. Sometimes heavy emotions do come in focusing, but a felt sense is always easier on the body than emotions.

Great passions, insane jealousy, tearing resentments, grand sufferings—these are sometimes patterns set off by little feelings you hardly noticed. Focus on the "little" feeling that set it off, especially if the strong passion is one you have many times felt and pursued already.

When people first hear of focusing, they sometimes assume that they would need a free afternoon for it in order to have overwhelming feelings and privately go to pieces for a while. Focusing is not like that. The felt sense of the whole thing feels *lighter* than what you are feeling already. You can focus while you are waiting for a bus. Just see what's between you and feeling fine. Don't go *into* these, just say "yes, that's there . . ." and feel the relief that comes from making the space. Then, if one problem needs working on, get the whole felt sense of it! "What is it like to have that there, now?" By the time you get on the bus you'll feel much better. The few minutes between things are good for focusing. Why carry your tensions around all day?

Focusing takes a few minutes, ten, fifteen, let's say even half an hour. But not more. Then it's time to talk, rest, do something else. Do not grind away at things. You will return later. Meanwhile, the body will process it.

Emotion Versus Felt Sense: This Distinction Is Vital

As you focus on a felt sense you may get further emotions coming out of it. But a felt sense is not an emotion like anger, fear, hate, joy, or anxiety. It is a sense of your *total* emotional situation, a feel of many things together, in which an emotion can be embedded or from which an emotion is produced.

Chapter 9
If You Can't Make Anything Shift

The body shift most often happens in the third, fourth, or fifth focusing movement. The third movement, you'll recall, is the one in which you get a handle for the quality of the felt sense, and the fourth is resonating back and forth between felt sense and handle. The fifth is the one in which you ask the felt sense what it is. (What about the whole problem makes this?) (In many people, as I've said, the three movements take place simultaneously or in such quick succession that there is no way—and of course, no need—to separate them.) If you get stuck in those movements, or can't seem to get into them at all, this chapter will offer some help.

Deliberate Letting-go

In the spectrum of people's attitudes toward their feelings, there are two opposite extremes that don't often produce useful results. One is the attitude of strict control: trying to make the head dominate the body, insisting that you won't give in to this or be stopped by that. The other extreme is that of never wanting to direct or control feelings, as if anything seems artificial except floating, letting images roam, letting feelings come and go.

Either extreme can prevent you from getting a body shift. Focusing is a deliberate, controlled process up to a certain point, and then there is an equally deliberate relaxation of control, a letting go, a dropping of the reins.

The very word "focusing" suggests that you are trying to make sharp what is at first vague. You grope down into a felt sense and you control the process to prevent yourself from drifting. "I want to know about *this* feeling, not any others right now," you tell yourself. "What's *this* feeling about? What's in it, what's underneath it?" If you do find yourself drifting, rein yourself back in: "Where was I just then? Ah...yes. I was at that stuff about guilt, or whatever it is. What is all *that* about?..."

Once you have made contact with a felt sense clearly and strongly, you drop the reins. Don't try to control what comes from it. *Let* what comes from the felt sense come: words, pictures, physical sensations, as long as it is *from* this felt sense.

The process might be called "deliberate letting-go."

Letting the Body Really Shift

When you first learn focusing, the bodily responses can be very slight. There is a barely noticeable "unhuh" in your body, when something comes that is just right. Learn to let your body take more of a shift. Try exhaling a deep long breath (like the many examples in this book where I have written "whew..."). Try nodding with your head. Try relaxing your whole body as if you had been sitting stiffly. This shift allows you to melt. If you do this purposely a few times, your body will learn to express itself more freely. Then don't do it on purpose any more, see what more expressive body moves come of their own accord.

As an example, think of a little girl who is very scared. She stands petrified, only her eyes moving. You walk up and say, "Honey, are you scared?" There is the barest little bit of a nod.

Now in this example, you know this little girl hasn't yet changed in her body. What you want is to say again to her: "Scared, honey? It's OK to feel whatever you feel, we'll see what we can do. Has it been scary?" The little girl might then practically melt in your arms, by way of saying "Yes, it *sure* has been scary."

Of course, there isn't always a major felt shift; sometimes a small step has only a slight bodily effect. But at times a major effect comes, if you don't settle too quickly for the barely noticeable "yes" in your body and keep asking it.

When something comes that feels correct in your body, check back a few times, not so much because it might be wrong but to let this more major bodily change happen.

Some Triggering Questions

When you have made contact with a felt sense but can't make it move, the problem may be only that you haven't yet asked yourself the right open-ended question. Sometimes feelings will respond to a question that is phrased in a certain way, but not to virtually the same question phrased another way. A question that makes things shift inside me one time might have no effect at another time. Thus it may help you to experiment with various phrasings until you find one or a few that work for you.

Listed below are the questions that seem to work most often in most people.

"What is this, really?" That is basically what you are trying to get at, but the question as phrased may be too general, too vague. These questions are more specific.

"What is the crux of this?"

"What is the worst of it?" Or "What are the two or three things about it that trouble me the most?"

"What is at the center of it?"

"What is under this? What is doing it?"

"What needs to happen for me with this?"

"What would it take to feel better?"

Notice that there are two basic kinds of questions: the kind that asks what's wrong, and the kind that asks what would be right. Another way to say it: we can ask into what the problem has been, or we can ask about what needs to happen and hasn't yet.

It is very important to ask the forward type of question sometimes.

For example, suppose you often feel lonely and isolated. When you focus, that feeling often comes. It is quite right to focus on what the whole felt sense is that goes with "isolated." You may find in what way you isolate yourself, or what quite different things this is really about. But it will be important at some point also to ask the felt sense: "What would it take not to feel this way?" or some question of that type.

Look for the life-steps forward, and not only at what the trouble has been.

When the Handle Fits
but Then You Are Stuck

You have made contact with the global felt sense of a problem and you have asked what the quality of it is. A handle has come: "I'm afraid." Seeking to go another step, you have asked what is under that fear, what is doing it. But nothing comes. All you can feel is "I'm scared," over and over again. You are stuck. What can you do?

Your problem may be that you have become stuck with a unit-label, which I mentioned in the last chapter. You are looking at the word—"scared," or whatever it may be—as though it says everything that needs to be said. Or you are locked onto "scared" as only that emotion. Let it broaden into a felt sense. What wider feeling does this "scared" come out of? There are a vast number of ways of feeling that can come along with "scared." Get a feel of this mass of feelings that go with *this* scared.

Or try a fresh start. Stand way back from the problem. It will remain there, don't worry. Take a break, take a breath. Then consider the problem as wider and deeper than just "scared." Bring home to yourself that it probably goes with much else in your life, your past, your future, other people, and so on. It is a whole slice of your life, a whole context. What is the whole sense in your body when you think of all that?

Or try, "Why am I scared?" Again don't answer. Keep saying the question and while you say it, try to get *the whole feel* of what goes along with this particular "scared." What are its unique qualities? Feel it inside you, and see what fresh words come from it. "I'm afraid... and there's a kind of loneliness with it, like I'm—Yes!

That's what it feels like! It's like I've been left stranded alone on a high scary place and everybody has gone away, and there's never going to be anybody to help me...."

Using Imagery

Another way to get a body shift when you are stuck is to let an image form. Many people have vivid imagery and many don't. But anyone can form an everyday image, even with open eyes. Try it: Imagine now the room where you sleep, and where your bed is. How do you get to the door from the bed? You can conjure a visual image of that even as you are reading.

In that same inner space, you can ask for an image of a feeling to form. Wait till it pops in. The image will express a felt sense. You might see a forest, for instance, a figure, a storm, a wall, yourself running.

When you have the image, then see how this image makes you feel. Often just having the image will shift something. Whether it does or not, ask yourself, "What does this image now make me feel?" It will probably give you a step.

Looking Up the Answer in the Back of the Book

If you cannot get a body shift, there is a different method, which lets your body experience what it *would* be like if the problem were resolved. Ask your body, "What would it feel like, in my body, if this difficulty somehow got completely resolved?" If you wait a few seconds you will feel the shift in your body.

It helps also, when you do this, to let your body shift outwardly, if it wants to. Perhaps your body will want to sit up with your head high, or perhaps it will want to relax and exhale, or move in some other way of its own accord.

By going through this process, you let your body give you a taste of what it will be like to feel right. When you reach that good feeling, keep it. See what you learn from it. After a while, tell yourself, "I can feel this way all the time." Then wait. If something new inside comes to you and says, "No. Sorry. You can't feel this way all the time," ask that "something" what it is.

This is much like prematurely looking up the answer to a math problem in the back of the book. You know what the answer looks like but not how to do the steps. But knowledge of the answer helps you to work backward. It lets you ask what is in the way, what you must change to get this answer. Working from the answer backward gives you steps you couldn't find from the problem.

Thus it is with this way of focusing. You let your body feel its answer. Not only does this feel good at the time you are doing it, but it lets you ask: "OK, what's in the way of feeling *this* way?"

That "what's in the way" can be a new opening. But to use it, you must pretend to yourself for a moment (knowing better, of course) that the problem really *is* all solved and you will remain in this good frame of mind-body.

Some people, when they ask what's in the way, go right back to where they were, the way they left the problem. Don't do that. Stay and pretend it's all solved until a *new* "what says no?" comes. You can do that by holding on to the good feeling, just as you would hold on to an answer from the back of the book while trying to make steps from it backwards.

Note an example from the later stages of someone's focusing:

"I sit with this bad feeling a while but it doesn't change. I know what it is, but that doesn't matter. What matters is I can't get it to shift. So I did this. 'What would your body feel like if it were all solved?' And I got 'Wow! I'd be free!' And my body sort of sat forward and my blood circulated more and I felt like moving my shoulders, like I was marching out into the world. It was a neat feeling! Then I said, 'OK, can I stay this way?' And it came and said 'No.' And I said, 'OK, why not?' and right away I got this special kind of being scared.

"It felt really good to focus on that special kind of scared, instead of the stuck bad feeling from before.

"That special scared, it turned out to be very odd. I wasn't scared of anything that's usual. I was scared of living, like I'd break something if I just came out, like living in a china store, sort of, that's the way I've been...."

Checking In

Make it a "place" you can leave and come back to. A painful place may not shift immediately. You may have to check in with its felt edge a number of times during the rest of the day, and perhaps for several days. Do it briefly and gently: "Can I still feel that whole thing? . . . Ah, there it is. Anything new? . . . Ah, still the same. OK." This takes only a minute. Eventually you will find a step or shift there.

Don't Say, "It Must Be . . ."

I want to warn you once more against analyzing, inferring, "figuring out." This can prevent anything from shifting. We all think we know much about our problems. We push our bodies around a great deal, try to force ourselves in this direction and that, guided by a Sunday school list of admired traits or by various social groups' lists of what are accepted as worthy goals. We don't listen to our bodies enough, and this failing can crop up even in the midst of focusing.

You might form a global felt sense of a problem, then grope for its crux and find it and feel good for a second or two. But then the old analyzing habit can take over. "Oh, sure, I know what this is about," you hear yourself say. "It must be . . ."

Whenever you hear phrases like "it must be," turn them off. You are only doing what most people do throughout their lives: trying to tell yourself what is wrong. Remember the importance of an "asking" rather than a "telling" internal attitude. Tell yourself nothing. Ask, wait, and let your body reply.

Your effectiveness in focusing, and the rewards it gives you, will improve with practice. In time, you won't need to think consciously about any of these troubleshooting rules. Nor, as I've said, will you need to think of the focusing process as a six-step exercise. It will become an easy and natural act, like walking.

And it will become a part of your everyday life, if you let it. You will find yourself using it not only in times of stress but as a help in solving all life's problems. Learn to trust your body's guidance.

PART THREE

People Helping
Each Other

Chapter 10
Finding Richness in Others

How many people do you really know? Your husband or wife? Your best friend? Your parents? It's probable that you don't really know even them. Sure, you know what they are likely to do under certain circumstances. What they always say, and what they are likely to go right on saying. You can probably imagine the next conversation you will have with them, and what you both will say. You'll come close to being right, but there is no opening up of inward experience.

Who really understands *you*? Who wants to hear what *you* feel? Most people will answer, "No one." Some few will say "So-and-so would like to hear it, but he can't understand me really." Very few people have someone they can share inner experience with, and then only up to a point. And even with yourself: have you not left certain places dark? Without even knowing just *why* you are scared of them? Or how you would go into them? Being so largely unknown and unseen makes us feel somewhat unreal, as if we exist only to ourselves and perhaps not quite even that.

We find that if listening and if focusing are shared, people can come to know each other more deeply in a few hours than most do in years.

Contact is a human need. Contact comes when we sense the difference we make to other people and they to us. Contact without really knowing each other (and our-selves through each other) is limited. We can huddle for warmth, get a little comfort, but too much privacy em-phasizes our isolation, even as we huddle together.

Authentic seeing and knowing each other comes with focusing and listening; inward experience opens up to ourselves. And if it doesn't open it cannot be seen and shared; it remains locked in its own dumb half-being.

Most people live without expressing their inner rich-ness. Much of what people do is canned routines, "roles." Sometimes they are alive in their roles, but more often not. Most often people have to keep themselves down, put themselves away, hold their breath till later. For many people there isn't much of a "later" either—and their inner selves become silent and almost disappear. They wonder if, inside, there is anything to them.

Even when we get into a relationship, much of it is the same thing: more roles and routines. We feel shattered and destroyed when they break because without them we are back to being alone.

Even when our relationships are "good," much of it exists in silence, or driving in a car saying, "Oh, look at that sign over there..."

Nor are the times of "openness" better. Usually it's a matter of the same torn and pained feelings expressed over and over again. Two people who are close tend to have the same feelings, year in and year out. To "speak openly" means saying and hearing the same stuck phrases from the same stuck places.

This chapter and the next will show you some ways to help closed, stuck relationships through focusing and *listening*.

At first, try the steps presented here with someone other than the person you're closest to. It need not always be the same person. The experience of contact and depth is easier to get at first with people who are not the most important to you.

Certainly you want to experience human beings in their inner reality. And, vice versa, you want the reality of being actually seen and taken in and sensed by another person as you really are.

We all know people with whom it is best not to share anything that matters to us. If we have experienced something exciting, and if we tell it to those people, it will seem almost dull. If we have a secret, we will keep it safe from those people, safe inside us, untold. That way it won't shrivel up and lose all the meaning it has for us.

But if you are lucky, you know one person with whom it is the other way around. If you tell that person something exciting, it becomes more exciting. A great story will expand, you will find yourself telling it in more detail, finding the richness of all the elements, more than when you only thought about it alone. Whatever matters to you, you save it until you can tell it to that person.

Focusing and listening are like that: like talking to a person who makes your experience expand. In focusing, you must be that kind of person within yourself. And you can also be that way with others, and show them how to be that way for you.

You will often want to focus alone. But also try it with someone else.

Suppose you want a friend to listen to you while and after you focus, and then help your friend focus, with you as listener. You may want to focus before approaching the friend, in order to find out just what your feelings are.

If you feel the relationship is close and easy, with lee-way for talking about deeply felt personal matters, you might find and say something like this: "I've just read this book, and it's about a kind of personal problem solving that sounds good. It says that it's easier to do with some-one else than alone. Let's divide the next hour—half for you, half for me. I think we might like to try it together. I thought I'd ask you because I found that [for example] I'm not scared of you, and I'm too scared to say anything about myself to most people."

You might point out that most of it can be done in si-lence. It's important to explain that people are asked to say about themselves only as much as they wish to say. Whoever is focusing or talking is in charge. The listener quietly waits while the other goes silently into feelings. If you explain the process to a friend this way, it won't sound difficult.

It is possible, right on the spot, to ask the person to pay attention to you for five minutes, and *not to say anything*. Then focus. When you shift, wait a few moments and say something general like: "I got a bad feeling, and just now I felt it easing up, and I see what the trouble was." Then be quiet another minute or so. Focus further until you get to a good stopping place. Sit up and remark (if true) that it was easier to focus this way than alone. Then ask if your friend would like to focus while you listen.

Now a surprising fact: focusing is easier with another person present, even though focuser and listener say nothing *at all*.

Usually, when I first ask people to give me their attention and company while I focus, I have to explain that I won't say anything much. I ask if that is all right. "Oh...," they say, and turn to pick up a newspaper or book. Then I have to explain that I need them to focus their attention on me, even though I won't be entertaining them with stories. At first they find it hard to believe that this could help, or that I could want such a thing. But the people who know how to focus also know this odd fact, and are quite glad both to give attention and to receive it.

It happens quite naturally. For example, an exchange like this is common:

"I feel grumpy and annoyed, and I have this work to do tonight, and I don't want to do it. Just can't make myself start."

"OK, can you go down to where it is, and see what it is?"

"Are you OK for a while, if I do that?"

"Yes, it's fine."

"OK." There is a long silence while the person focuses. Then: "Whew...I feel better. I got what it is."

"Are you OK now, or is it not completely OK yet?"

"I think it's OK for now. Thanks! How are *you?*"

It might surprise you that this exchange actually occurred during a long-distance call between Chicago and New York! Neither person thought it the slightest bit odd to take up five long-distance minutes with the silence of focusing.

In the above example the person who focused chose not to talk during the focusing. But this need not be so.

As we've already seen, in many focusing sessions some talk may go on. More often, it's before or after silent focusing that people may wish to talk at length.

Now let's discuss how to be a good listener. It sounds simpler than it is. Few people are, in fact, good listeners, and this judgment includes most psychotherapists, social workers, teachers, vocational counselors, and others whose professions should require of them that they listen well. I hope the *Listening Manual*, which follows, will also be read and studied by professionals and people who are not in the "listening" professions.

You will find it helpful to read both this and the *Focusing Manual* aloud, with another person or a group. Even though I was part of writing the manuals, it still helps me when someone reads them to me.

Chapter 11
The Listening Manual[1]

Four kinds of helping are discussed here, used at different times for different purposes. Be sure to become competent with the first before you try the others. Once you learn them and they become part of your way of dealing with people, you will find yourself using each of them in situations that are appropriate to each.

The First Kind of Helping: Helping Another Person Focus While Talking

A. Absolute listening[2] If you set aside a period of time when you only listen, and indicate only whether you follow or not, you will discover a surprising fact. People can tell you much more and also find more inside themselves, than can ever happen in ordinary interchanges.

If you use only expressions such as "Yes," or "I see," or "Oh yes, I can sure see how you feel," or "I lost you, can you say that again, please?" you will see a deep process unfold.

In ordinary social interchange we nearly always stop

---

1. *The Listening Manual* was written with Mary Hendricks, with the aid of Allan Rohlfs and others.

2. The method of "saying back" was discovered by Carl Rogers.

each other from getting very far inside. Our advice, reactions, encouragements, reassurances, and well-intentioned comments actually prevent people from feeling understood. Try following someone carefully without putting anything of your own in. You will be amazed.

Give the speaker a truthful sense of when you follow, and when not. Immediately you will be a good listener. But you must be truthful and indicate when you fail to follow. ("Can you say that another way? I didn't get it.")

However, it helps much more if you the listener will *say back* the other person's points, step by step, as you understand them. I call that *absolute listening.*

Never introduce topics that the other person didn't express. Never push your own interpretations. Never mix in your own ideas.

There are only two reasons for speaking while listening: to show that you understand exactly by saying back what the other person has said or meant, or to ask for repetition or clarification.

To show that you understand exactly   Make a sentence or two that gets at the personal meaning this person *wanted to put across.* This will usually be in your own words, but use that person's own words for the touchy main things.

People need to hear you speak. They need to hear that you got each step. Make a sentence or two for every main point they make, for each thing they are trying to get across. (Usually, this will be for about every five or ten sentences of theirs.) Don't just "let them talk," but relate to each thing that they feel, whether it's good or bad.

Don't try to fix or change or improve it. Try to get the crux of it exactly the way they mean it and feel it.

Sometimes what people say is complicated. You can't get what they say, nor what it means to them, all at once. First, make a sentence or two about the crux of what they said. Check that out with them. Let them correct it and add to it if they want to. Take in, and say back, what they have changed or added, until they agree that you have it just as they feel it. Then make another sentence to say what it means to them, or how they feel it.

Example: Suppose a woman has been telling you about some intricate set of events, what some people did to her and how and when, to "put her down."

First, you would say one or more sentences to state in words the crux of what she said as she sees it. Then she corrects some of how you said it, to get it more exactly. You then say back her corrections: "Oh, so it wasn't that they all did that, but all of them *agreed* to it." Then she might add a few more things, which you again take in and say back more or less as she said them. Then, when you have it just right, you make another sentence for the personal meaning or feeling that whole thing has: "And what's really bad about it is that it's made you feel put down."

If you don't understand what the person is saying, or you get mixed up or lost There is a way to ask for repetition or clarification. Don't say, "I didn't understand any of it." Rather, take whatever bits you did understand, even if it was very vague, or only the beginning, and use it to ask for more:

"I do get that this is important to you, but I don't get what it is yet...."

Don't say a lot of things you aren't sure the person meant. The person will have to waste lots of time explaining to you why what you said doesn't fit. Instead, just say what you are sure you heard and ask them to repeat the rest.

Say back *bit by bit* what the person tells you. Don't let the person say more than you can take in and say back. Interrupt, say back, and let the person go on.

How you know when you are doing it right   You know this when people go further into their problems. For example, the person may say, "No, it's not like that, it's more like—uh—" and then may feel further into it to see how it actually feels. You have done it right. Your words may have been wrong, or may now sound wrong to the person even though they were very close to what the person said a moment before. But what matters is that your words led the person to feel further into the problem so your words had the right result. Whatever the person *then* says, take *that* in and say it back. It's a step further.

Or the person may sit silently, satisfied that you get everything up to now.

Or the person may show you a release, a relaxing, a whole-bodied "Yes, that's what it is," a deep breath, a sigh. Such moments occur now and then, and after them new or further steps come.

You may also tell that it is going right by more subtle signs of the relaxation that comes from being heard well—the feeling we all get when we have been trying to say something and have finally put it across: the feeling that we don't have to say *that* any more. While a person is laying out an idea, or part of one, there is a tension, a holding of breath, which may remain for several interchanges. When the crux is finally both said and exactly understood and responded to, there is relaxation, like an exhaling of breath. The person doesn't have to hold the thing in the body any more. Then something further can come in. (It's important to accept the silence that can come here for what seems like a long time, even a minute or so. The focuser now has the inner body peace to let another thing come up. *Don't destroy the peace by speaking needlessly.*)

How you know when you did it wrong, and what to do about that If nearly the same thing is said over again, it means the person feels you haven't got it yet. See how the focuser's words differ from what you said. If nothing feels different, then say it again and add to it, "But that's not all, or that's not right, some way?"

As you respond, the focuser's face may get tight, tense, confused. This shows that the focuser is trying to understand what you are saying. So you must be doing it wrong, adding something or not getting it. Stop and ask the person again to say how it is.

If the focuser changes the subject (especially to something less meaningful or less personal), it means he or she gave up on getting the more personal thing across right. You can interrupt and say something like, "I'm still with what you were just trying to say about . . . I know I didn't understand it right, but I want to." Then say only the part of it you're sure of, and ask the person to go on from there.

You will get it right sooner or later. *It doesn't matter when.* It can be the third or fourth try. People can get further into their feelings best when another person is receiving or trying to receive each bit exactly as they have it, without additions or elaborations. There is a centeredness that is easy to recognize after a while. Like a train on a track. It's easy to know when you're off. Everything stops. If that happens, go back to the last point that was on a solid track inside, and ask the person to go on from there.

If you find it hard to accept someone with unlovely qualities, think of the person as being *up against* these qualities inside. It is usually easy to accept the person inside who is struggling against these very qualities. As you listen, you will then discover that person.

When you first practice listening, be sure to repeat almost word for word what people say. This helps you see how hard it is to get what a person is trying to say without adding to it, fixing it, putting yourself into it.

When you are able to do that, then feed back only the crux, the point being made, and the feeling words.

To make it easier, stop for a second and sense your own tangle of feelings, tensions, and expectations. Then clear this space. Out of this open space you can listen. You will feel alert and probably slightly excited. What will the other person *say* into this waiting space that exists for nothing except to be spoken into?

Very rarely is anyone offered such a space by another person. People hardly ever move over in themselves enough to really hear another.

B. Helping a felt sense form It is possible for a person to focus a little between one communication and the next. Having made a point, and being understood, the person can focus before saying the next thing.

Most people don't do that. They run on from point to point, only talking.

How can you help people stop, and get the felt sense of what they have just said?

This is the second focusing movement. Finding the felt sense is like saying to oneself, "That, right there, *that's* what's confused," and *then feeling it there.*

The focuser must keep quiet, not only outwardly but also inside, so that a felt sense can form. It takes as long as a minute.

Some people talk all the time, either out loud or at themselves inside. Then nothing directly felt can form, and everything stays a painful mass of confusion and tightness.

When a felt sense forms, the focuser feels relief. It's as if all the bad feeling goes into one spot, right there, and the rest of the body feels freer.

Once a felt sense forms, people can relate to it. They can wonder what's *in* it, can feel around it and into it.

When to help people let a felt sense form   When people have said all that they can say clearly, and from there on it is confusing, or a tight unresolved mess, and they don't know how to go on.

When there is a certain spot that you sense could be gone into further.

When people talk round and round a subject and never go down into their feelings of it. They may start to say things that are obviously personal and meaningful, but then go on to something else. They tell you nothing meaningful, but seem to want to. In this very common situation, you can interrupt the focuser and gently point out the way into deeper levels of feeling.

FOCUSER: "I've been doing nothing but taking care of Karen since she's back from the hospital. I haven't been with me at all. And when I do get time now, I just want to run out and do another chore."

LISTENER: "You haven't been able to be with yourself for so long, and even when you can now, you don't."

FOCUSER: "She needs this and she needs that and no matter what I do for her it isn't enough. All her family are like that. It makes me angry. Her father was like that, too, when he was sick, which went on for years. They're always negative and grumpy and down on each other."

LISTENER: "It makes you angry the way she is, the way they are."

FOCUSER: "Yes. I'm angry. Damn right. It's a poor climate. Living in a poor climate. Always gray. Always down on something. The other day, when I—"

LISTENER (interrupts): "Wait. Be a minute with your angry feeling. Just feel it for a minute. See what more is in it. Don't think anything. . . ."

How to help a felt sense form   There is a gradation of how much help people need to contact a felt sense.

Always do the least amount first, and more only if that doesn't work.

Some people won't need any help except your willingness to be silent. If you don't talk all the time, and if you don't stop them or get them off the track, they will feel into what they need to feel into. Don't interrupt a silence for at least a minute. Once you have responded and checked out what you said and gotten it exactly right, be quiet.

The person may need one sentence or so from you, to make the pause in which a felt sense could form. Such a sentence might simply repeat slowly the last important word or phrase you already said. It might just point again to that spot. For instance, in the previous example you might have said slowly and emphatically: "Really angry." Then you would stay quiet. The person's whole sense of all that goes with being angry should form.

Whatever people say after your attempt to help them find a felt sense, say the crux of it back. Don't worry if you can't immediately create the silent deeper period you feel is needed. You can try it again soon. Go along with whatever comes up, even if the focuser has wandered off the track momentarily.

If after many tries the people still aren't feeling into anything, then you can tell them to do so more directly. Say explicitly, "Sit with it a minute and feel into it further." You can also give all or some of the focusing instructions.

You can form a question for people. Tell them to ask this question inwardly, to ask not the head but the gut. "Stay quiet and don't answer the question in words. Just wait with the question till something comes from your feeling."

Questions like that are usually best open-ended. "What really *is* this?" "What's keeping this the way it is?"

Another type of question applies to the "whole thing." "Where am I really hung up in this whole thing?" Use it when everything is confused or when the focuser doesn't know how to begin.

If the focuser has let a felt sense form but is still stuck, it may help to ask, "How would it be different if it were all OK? What ought it to be like?" Tell the person to feel that ideal state for a while and then ask, "What's in the way of that?" The focuser shouldn't try to answer the question but should get the feel of what's in the way.

All these ways require that the focuser stop talking, both out loud and inside. One *lets what is there come* instead of doing it oneself.

Just ask, "Where's my life still hung up?" This will give you the felt sense of the problems fast, if you don't answer with words.

Another approach: pick the two or three most important things the focuser has said if you feel they go together into one idea. Then tell the person, "When I say what I'm going to say, don't you say anything to me or to yourself. Just feel what comes there." Then say the two or three things, each in one or two words.

These ways can also help when a person doesn't want to say some private or painful thing. The focuser can work on it without actually telling you what it is. You can listen and help without knowing what it is about, beyond the fact that it hurts or puzzles in some way.

How you can tell when it isn't working When people look you straight in the eyes, then they aren't yet focusing in-

side themselves. Say, "You can't get into it while you're looking at me. Let me just sit here while you go into yourself."

If people speak immediately after you get through
asking them to be quiet, they haven't focused yet. First,
say back the crux of what was said and then ask the focuser to contact the felt sense of it. If you've worked hard
on it and nothing useful has happened, let it go fifteen
minutes or so and try again.

If, after a silence, the person comes up with explanations and speculations, ask how that problem *feels*. Don't
criticize the person for analyzing. Pick up on what the
person does say and keep pointing into a felt sense of it.

If people say they can't let feeling come because they
are too restless or tense, feel empty or discouraged, or are
trying too hard, ask them to focus on *that*. They can ask
themselves (and not answer in words), "What is this rat-
tled feeling?" "... or tense feeling?" "... or empty feeling?"
"... or 'trying too hard' thing?"

How to tell when a person has a felt sense One has a
felt sense when one can feel more than one understands,
when what is there is more than words and thoughts,
when something is quite definitely experienced but is not
yet clear, hasn't opened up or released yet.

You will know your focuser has a felt sense and is referring to it when that person gropes for words and evidently has something that is not yet in words.

Anything that comes in this way should be welcomed.
It is the organism's next step. Take it and say it back just
the way the person tells it.

It feels good to have something come directly from one's
felt sense. It shifts the feelings, releases the body slightly.

Even if one doesn't like what has come, it feels good. It is encouraging when more is happening than just talk. It gives one a sense of process, freeing from stuck places.

This is the key concept in this process of listening, responding, and referring to people's feelings just as *they* feel them. It is based on the fact that feelings and troubles are not just concepts or ideas: they are bodily. Therefore the point of helping is never just to speculate, to explain. There has to be a physical process of steps into where the trouble is felt in the body. Such a process gets going when a good listener responds to the personal, felt side of anything said, just as the person feels it, without adding anything. Felt movement and change happen when a person is given the peace to allow the bodily sense of a trouble to be, to be felt, and to move to its own next step.

A focuser can do this alone, but the presence and response of another person has a powerful helping effect.

The Second Kind of Helping: Using Your Own Feelings and Reactions About the Other Person

There are ways of doing more than listening, but they aren't "more" if you do them without listening!

In this section I will show you how to try out many other things, but in a way that always keeps listening as basic.

Try some of them, one at a time, and then go right back to listening for a while.

How to say your reaction   Whatever you say or do, watch the person's face and respond to how your input affects the person. If you can't see that, ask. Even if what you say or do is stupid and hurtful, it will work out well if you then ask about and say back whatever the person's reaction to it is. Switch back to listening right after saying your own reaction.

Make your statements questions, not conclusions. And direct your questions to people's feelings, not just their ideas. Invite people to go into themselves and see whether they feel something like what you say—or something else. You don't ever *know* what they feel. You only wonder and help them to ask themselves. You might say, "I don't mean that *I* would know. Feel it out and see. Is it like that, or just how is it?"

Note that the person must feel what is there, to answer your question, if you put it this way.

Let go of your idea easily as soon as you see that it leads into arguments or speculation, or just doesn't get further into anything directly felt. If you think it's good you can say it twice, but after that, abandon it. You can bring it up later. (You could be right but something else might have to come first.)

Make sure that there are stretches of time when you do total listening. If you interrupt with your ideas and re-actions constantly, the basic focusing process can't get going. There should be ten or fifteen minutes at a time when you should only listen. If the person is feeling into his or her problem, do less talking; if the person is stuck, do more.

Let the person's process go ahead if it seems to want to move a certain way. Don't insist that it move into what *you* sense should be next.

If the person tries to teach you to be a certain way, be

that way for a while. For instance, some people might express a need to have you more quiet or more talkative, or to work with them in some definite way. Do it. You can always go back to your preferred way later. People often teach us how to help them.

If you find you have gotten things off a good track and into confusion, bring the process back to the last point where the focuser was in touch with feelings. Say, "You were telling me . . . go on from there."

Watch your person's face and body, and if you see something happening, ask about it. Nonverbal reactions are often good signals to ask people to get them into a felt sense.

For instance, the focuser might say, "That happened but I feel OK about it." You respond, "You feel OK about it in some way. But I see from the way your foot is tapping, and the way you look, that something might not be OK, too. Is that right?"

You don't need to get hung up on whether you're right or not when you sense something. If you sense something, then there is *something*, but you may not be right about *what* it is. So ask.

You will often see the focuser's face reacting to whatever you are saying or doing. Ask about that, too.

Feel easy about it if the person doesn't like what you're doing. You can change it, or you might not need to. Give the person room to have negative reactions to you, and listen and say back what they are.

Don't always stay with the words the person is saying. Does the voice sound angry? Discouraged? Insistent? Is there a sudden break in it? *What way* were the words said? Ask: "You sound angry. Are you?" And if the answer is yes, ask what that is about. If the focuser gets no further, ask: "Can you sense what the anger is?"

You can use your own felt reactions to what's going on to help you sense more clearly what is going on with the other person or with both of you. If you feel bored, annoyed, impatient, angry, embarrassed, excited, or any way that stands out, it indicates something. Focus on what it is in you. If you are bored, you might find that it is because the person isn't getting into anything meaningful. Then you can ask: "Are you getting into what you really want to get into?" If you are angry, what is the person doing to make you angry? When you find that, you can say it. For instance: "Are you maybe shutting me out because you gave up on my helping you. Did you?"

Let yourself have any feelings at all while working with someone. Let them be as unlovely and as honest as they can be. That way you can be free inside to attend to what's happening in you. That often points to what's happening with the other person or between the two of you.

If you get an idea as to what someone is feeling by putting together a lot of theoretical reasoning or a long set of hints, don't take up time explaining all this to the other person. Just ask whether the person can find the feeling you inferred.

You can express any hunch or idea as a question. Sometimes you might add another possibility to insure that the focuser knows it's not a conclusion but an invitation to look within at the feeling itself. "Is it like you're scared...or maybe ashamed? How does it feel?" Then listen.

In the rest of this second section on helping I offer

many reactions that you might say to help someone. You needn't read and grasp these all right now. You can look these up when you have become competent in listening and want more ideas to try. For now, you should probably move on to the third kind of helping.

Some questions to create movement It is often worthwhile (though not always feasible) to ask if the focuser's sex life is good. If it is not, it may help to see if sexual needs are felt as frightening or bad. It may also help to talk about what's standing in the way of a good sex life, as well as how to change situations or get into new ones. (Some people may find such questions nosy or silly. Don't ask unless you are sure that your focuser will accept your asking.)

"Crazy" conditions are often related to one's life situation. If your rapport with the person is such that a question about private matters doesn't seem shocking or nosy, or if the person mostly speaks of strange or hallucinatory stuff, try asking if the person has friends, work, places to go, sexuality. The person can focus on these with or without telling you all the details.

Feelings are inside and "relationships" are outside. But inside and outside are always related, and a good listener can help a troubled focuser find steps to change the outside, too.

You can ask people, referring to any bad thing they are fighting or puzzling over inside: "How is this bad thing in some way good, or useful, or sensible?" This is a complex, profound question, and you might precede it with something like this: "No bad thing that's in a person is *all* bad. If it's there, it has or might have some right or useful aspect that we have to listen for. If we find what the thing is good for, then it can let go. So give it a friendly hearing and see what it says, why it's right." The point is to help the focuser stop fighting the undesired ways long enough to allow them to open, so the positive aspect in them can come out.

Often a troubled inner state protects us from other painful problems. If we can see what a painful thing protects us from, we can sometimes protect ourselves much better than the thing itself can.

Sometimes a person's trouble lies in the fighting against the way the body feels. If you let how you feel simply be, a positive next step can then come out of it—one that you couldn't make up and force.

Sometimes it helps to ask a suicidal person: "Are you thinking about committing suicide *at* somebody? At *whom*?" (By this I mean attempting to hurt someone by committing suicide.) The focuser may know right away, and the focus may then shift to where it needs to—that relationship. It may help also to say that the other person in that relationship probably won't understand the focuser's suicide attempt any better than the person ever understood anything else.

Sometimes, if a person is angry, it pays to ask: "Are you hurt about something?"

Sometimes you can ask: "Do you feel that you can't *ever* get what you need?" (If so, let the focuser feel into what that is.) Some people's most frantic, seemingly destructive reactions are really a life-affirming fight against some part in them that forbids what they need ever to come about. The point then is to shift the focus to this assumption or prohibition, which has to be false in some way. What does it say, and why?

If a feeling keeps being there, over and over, you can ask the person to "switch roles"[1] with the feeling. The person stands up, loosens the body, and prepares as if to act a role on stage. The role is to *be* the feeling. "Wait... sense it in your body, what would this feeling do to you, how would it act, what would it say, how would it stand or move? Wait and see what comes in your body."

Sometimes body expressions, crying, or yelling certain words arise spontaneously. When that has finished happening, it is important to find and focus on the felt sense that these expressive "discharges" come out of.

Some suggestions to point people in a forward direction It helps to assure people that it's OK to have their feelings—at least long enough to feel what they are. The same is true of needs, desires, ways of seeing things. There are various reasons people stay clear of their feelings, as we've seen. Among the reasons: the fear that bad feeling will lead to destructive actions.

If someone is afraid of feelings, you might say:

"Feelings and actions aren't the same thing. You can let yourself feel whatever you do feel. Then you can still decide what you choose to *do*.

"It's OK to need. Trying not to have a need that you do in fact have makes a lot of trouble. Even if you can't get it, don't fight needing it.

---

1. The "switch roles" method was invented by Fritz Perls. Here it is done in a focusing way.

"Focusing isn't like just wallowing around in what you feel. Don't sink into it, stay next to it. Let yourself feel whatever is there and expect it to open up.

"Weird states are different from feelings. It helps to move out of them toward life and ordinary situations. Weird states may not ease by getting further into them. What in your life is making things bad? What happens if you lean forward into living, instead of lying back?"

If the person suddenly feels weird or unreal, slow down. Take a short break. Ask the person to look around the room, recall the ordinary to the person's attention. Then continue.

But *you* shouldn't decide whether the focuser should go into, or out of, anything. The focuser should decide. Your company may be wanted in probing some weird thoughts—or may not.

"To change something or do something that's been too hard, we have to find a small first step you can actually do. What would that be?" Suggest small first steps if the focuser has none, but don't settle on anything unless it is received with some elation that that first step is possible. "Can you make a list of places to go meet new people? As a first step, make a list."

Some people are so concerned with what somebody else thinks that they need help getting to what they themselves think and feel.

"Put away for a minute what *they* think and what *they* said, and let's see what *you* feel about it, how *you* see it."

Dealings with very troubled people You can talk about yourself, your day—anything you feel like saying. You need not always try to get into the other person's problems. Of course, if the focuser is in the midst of talking about them or seems to want to, you should not then refuse to listen. The person should know you would listen. But there will be times when it will be a relief to a troubled person to find that you can just talk of other things.

Silent, peaceful times are also useful. It is good to lie on the grass, go for a walk, without any tension of waiting for something to be said.

You can even get very troubled people to talk about (or do) something they happen to be competent in—for example, sewing or music. This helps them feel OK for a while and lets you respond to a competent person— respond positively and for good reason.

It is often after such times, after having been able to just be with you, that a person might feel like taking you into some areas that are disturbing.

If the person talks a lot about strange material you can't understand and then says one or two things that make sense, stick with those and repeat them many times.[1] They are your point of contact. It is all right to keep returning to these phrases, with silence or other topics in between, for as long as an hour.

If the person says things that can't be true, respond to the feeling rather than to the distorted facts or untruths. For example, "The Martians took everything I had away from me...." You can get the feeling here. Say, "Somebody took what was yours?"

---

1. This "reiteration" method was developed by Garry Prouty.

Other ways to be helpful Let's say a man asks you for something you can't give. You may have to refuse the request itself, but you can tell him you're glad he's in touch with what he needs. Tell him you're glad he felt free to ask. This is especially so if the need is in the direction of life and growth for the person, if for the first time he can allow himself to want or ask for closeness or time with you.

When a person acts toward you in a way that is obviously destructive or self-defeating (and you think, no wonder lots of people dislike this person), there are several things you can do:

1. You can say how it makes you feel.
2. You can point to what the person is doing and ask what that feels like inside. Leave it vague, not defined. If you call it "attacking," "manipulating," "lazy," "whining," "controlling," or any such condemning label, you give only the external view. Inside the focuser it's something more complex. So be puzzled about what this is, even if you can give it a clear disapproving name from your outside perspective.
3. If you sense what a good life-thrust might be in this bad way of acting, then respond to that life-thrust. A lot of bad ways are bad only because the right thing is being *half* done, instead of being done fully and freely. If you respond to the half of it that *is* happening, that lets it happen more. Responding to the half that's missing isn't as helpful.

Example: Someone is whiningly complaining. It would not be helpful to say, "Why do you always whine and come on so weak? Why don't you stand up for yourself and say what you want?" It is more helpful to respond to the positive half of this that's trying to happen, and say, "You're saying what you need from people, and calling a halt to what they've been doing."

Some healthy life-enhancing processes are: taking up for yourself, defending the way you see it, allowing yourself to be free to feel as you do, reaching out for someone, trying to do something that you haven't been able to for some time, exploring, wondering about yourself, trying to meet people, sexuality, a sense of cosmic significance or mystery, seeking peace, letting someone see you, trying something new, taking charge of a situation, telling people how you need them to be, being honest, hoping, refusing to give up, being able to ask for help. These are all good life-thrusts.

No one should depend on just you alone. Let the person meet other people you know, or call someone else in to help, if the person lacks others.

The person should be present when being discussed by people trying to help. It's hard to be straight in front of someone you're trying to help, but we've already seen why you must.

A person's needs for help with a job, a place to live, and so on, should be part of what help is about. Help is about needs, whatever they may be. It's not useful to separate "psychological" problems from the rest. They aren't separate in a person's life.

The Third Kind of Helping: Interaction

Until now you were either saying back the other person's feelings (the first kind) or giving your feelings and ideas about the other person's feelings (the second). Up to now it was all about helping the other person. Now we come to *your* feelings. This section is as much for you as for helping the other person. Ideally, both can profit equally.

Our feelings, when we are with others, are often about those others. And yet they are our own feelings. We often feel like blaming the other person for our feelings:

"I feel that you're very defensive."

"I feel that you're manipulating me."

"I feel angry because you always interrupt me."

"I feel disappointed because you don't feel any better."

In these examples we express our feelings by saying that the other person is no good, behaves badly, or is the reason for our feelings. To express our feelings in a more useful way we must *focus* into them and get in touch with what's in *us*. These feelings will still relate to what the other person did, but they will be strictly our feelings and not the other person's burden. For example:

> "It's always hard for me to keep a train of thought, or keep feeling it's worth saying. So when you interrupt me, it hits my weak spot. I get so I can't make room for myself to say things to you. That's why it makes me angry.
>
> "I have sort of a stake in being a big help to people. I guess I'm disappointed that you're not feeling better. I do care about you too, but I see that my disappointment is my own thing. I need to be Big Helper."

How to express yourself From a given moment of interaction you can move either into the other person or into yourself. For example, let's say you are with a woman who has done something to upset you. You can go from this into what she did and what she is like and why she did it. Or you can go into what you are like and how it upsets you.

Don't do the first. Leave that to the other person. Do the second: move from the bit of interaction into your own feelings. See why it affected you and share this.

It is hard for people to hear you say what's wrong with them. It is easy to listen to you saying what's wrong with you, or what is at any rate vulnerable or upsettable or shaky in you. Avoid making comments that start, "I feel that you..." You're invading the other's territory and protecting yours.

Sharing what is happening *in you* makes the interaction more open and personal. The other person can then feel comfortable about sharing inner things with you.

Don't say:

"I have to express my feelings. Can I trust you with it? I feel you bully me."

Do say:

"I get angry and upset when I can't get to finish what I started to say. I lose track. I get insecure about whether I have any real ideas."

It is essential to be specific in expressing yourself. Avoid generalities. It is still a rebuke to a person to be told he or she made you upset. It is not real sharing when you share only a generality. But if you share some of the specifics actually going on in you—your unique felt sense of the situation—you share yourself. You can find these specifics by focusing at that moment.

Be ready to stand it if what you share is ignored. The other person may not be able to meet you immediately, may still be in some private anger or withdrawal, and may lag behind you in being open. The person may have to say angry things once or twice more, or laugh derisively. Your openness will be apparent, but the person may be unable to meet it. So don't expect *immediate* warm receptiveness as feedback. If you feel shaky, wait until what you say can stand on its own, whatever the other's reaction.

It is better to say, "I'm mad," than to say angry things and let your anger be seen indirectly. Saying your feeling directly lets it be shared.

If the first words that come to you feel hard to say, don't fight with yourself. Wait a few moments and let another string of words form. Do this till you get words that feel OK to say. Don't give up whatever needs expressing.

Focus directly on what you most fear, or what you find yourself struggling with. If what the other person says makes you uptight, pay attention to what you're afraid is being said and what you're afraid that means. Then say the crux of what you find inside.

We often work desperately on the surface of what we feel, or how we've just reacted, trying to fix it or make it be something else. But it is easy to let the real feeling speak directly.

Examples:

"That hurts my feelings."
"I'm hurt that you're angry."

"That makes me feel pushed away."
"I feel outmaneuvered."
"I'm stuck."

Say explicitly the covert things that go on in interaction, and say how you feel about them. Often things are happening that both of you can feel, but that both hope aren't being noticed.

For example, the other person might be pressuring you, and you might be trying to avoid being pushed into something while trying not to let on that you are resisting. Or you might have done something stupid or wrong, and you might be trying to recoup without that error being acknowledged, trying to make it be something other than it was.

When things like this have really occurred, saying them gets things unstuck. Not saying them keeps the interaction stuck.

Talk about it if you did something and now wish you hadn't. It may seem too late, but it's never too late to get the interaction unstuck.

Examples:

"I feel stupid about getting mad and yelling."
"Back a while ago, you said . . . and I said yes. I was too chicken to say no. I was afraid of fighting it out with you."

What feels impossible to face up to often provides a special opportunity to become closer to someone.

If nothing is happening and you wish something would—even if it seems that not much is going on in you—focus. There are always many things going on there, and some of them belong with the interaction with this person. Express them.

When you are being pushed too far, call a halt, set a limit. Do this before you blow up or get mad. Protect the other person from what happens when you don't take care of your needs. Say what you want or don't want, while you still have the time and concern to stay and hear what it means to the other person.

For example:

"I like it that I'm helpful when you call me up, but now it's happening too often. So instead of feeling good about it, like I used to, I feel pushed. I'd like to feel good about your calling. If I knew you'd call only twice a week, I know I'd like it again."

You are not trying to get rid of the person. You make the limits firm, so that within those limits you can feel good about the person again.

Having set these limits, you would stay to hear how the other person feels about them.

If you are sitting with a silent person, say something like, "I'll just sit here and keep you company." Relax. Show that you can maintain yourself on your own without needing to be dealt with. In such a silence, if it's long, you will have many chains of feelings, some of which you can express (every few minutes, perhaps).

Do not tell feelings you haven't got and only wish you had. Tell anything valuable you do have. If you find it painful to be honest, realize that other people don't care how good or wise or beautiful you are. Only you care all that much. It is not harmful to the other person if you look stupid or imperfect.

What is true is already so. Owning up to it doesn't make it worse. Not being open about it doesn't make it go away. And because it's true, it is what *is* there to be interacted with. Anything untrue isn't there to be lived. People can stand what is true, for they are already enduring it.

When not to express yourself   Be silent when people are focusing or talking about their concerns, or might if you made room. Delay articulating your side. People can almost always hear you better if they are heard first, and get in touch with where they are first. Also, as the other person does this, it may change what you feel without your saying anything. It might be hard to let the other person go first. But if the other person is full of unclear and upsetting feelings, you might not be heard unless you wait.

If you are very upset, and if the interaction isn't already a trusting one, wait a few moments before expressing yourself. As you calm down you can sift your feelings better. Also they are easier for the other person to experience if it seems clear that you aren't being wiped out by what you feel.

Don't express yourself immediately if you are confused about what you feel, and will only skirt your deepest feelings. Focus to learn what they are.

When to express yourself   Express yourself when you want to make a relationship closer.

Or when you are being "twisted out of your own shape" in some way. For instance, speak up if the person is implying that you feel some way you don't really feel.

Then listen again. It is all right if the person doesn't believe you if you have been heard. Don't argue.

Also express yourself when the other person needs to hear more from you to feel at ease about you, or has misconstrued one of your reactions. Say openly how it is with you. Don't let the other try to relate to what you really were not feeling. Even though it may be easier for you to remain unseen, misunderstood, and unapproachable, no interaction is possible if you do.

When you are in a group and nothing is happening, express something about yourself. This opens things up for others to express themselves. Give them something personal and meaningful from within you.

When the other person isn't up to relating with you, it may help if you just freely express anything about yourself. This way you don't have to be carried by the other's energy.

Express yourself when you are being idealized. Share some personal trouble or not-so-nice feeling you find in yourself.

Express yourself when the other person worries about having wounded or destroyed you. Give the specifics of how you do feel. Let it be seen that, although hurt or upset, you are not destroyed.

Express yourself when you just feel like it. There are two people here. You have equal rights. You may not always need to know why you feel like expressing yourself.

The Fourth Kind of Helping: Interacting in a Group

What follows concerns any group. It might be a staff meeting or your family. It might be a social group or a task group. It might be a group set up specifically for focusing—something I will discuss in a later chapter.

We have all heard that groups should "process," take up openly bad feelings. Usually that doesn't work very well. People hurt each other's feelings and don't really resolve them. Everyone gets a say, but no one can go very many steps. No one is really listened to, or focuses, so that the feelings can *change*. Yet this is what is needed, and can happen. But it usually happens only with listening and focusing.

Focusing can happen in a group, however large. Someone reads the instructions and everyone focuses within the silences between.

Afterwards there should be a time when each person can say something. If the group is large, it can divide into small groups. Divide the available time, and have someone with a watch call time for each person. Say you have half an hour and ten people. Each person gets two and a half minutes (leaving time lost in between). When people ramble, two and a half minutes is nothing, but if they know the time in advance, and have focused, it may be more time than some people will use. Take a minute or two in silence to let people decide approximately what they will say.

A warm group climate exists when people are free to say only what they wish, and no one criticizes, edits, or adds anything whatsoever to it. If people are skilled in listening, or listening is being taught, the person on the right can respond listeningly. If people are not skilled or learning listening, then no one should say anything except the person whose turn it is.

When the group is having trouble with someone, or

you are having trouble with someone, set aside a separate time and arrange for a few people to talk with the person. With just a few people meeting, each can be fully heard and be given enough time. Let the purpose be everybody's growth and straightness. Difficulties between people and within people don't impede the work and dynamics of the group. If they're dealt with in this way, they make a group better. When problems get resolved, and any person in the group experiences growth, the others feel the excitement.

If several people talk with someone who is upset or upsetting, at least one should be designated to insure that the person gets really listened to. This helps the person cope with disturbing feedback from other group members.

Credit another person with some good or seemingly good reasons for whatever is psychologically upsetting or harmful, even if you feel angry or find the person unreasonable.

When an interaction is bad and continues to be bad— say you've been talking for ten minutes and it's getting worse—stop. Go to the first and second stages of listening. Assume the other person is trying to do some good thing. Say that. Try to find what this good thing is and say it. (If you don't like it, you can say that you don't agree but that you do understand.) Then, when the other person's side is cleared or heard, say you now want to do your side, and do it. Even if the person doesn't want to hear it, say your side before it's over, or sometime soon. Perhaps bring in someone who can help you be heard.

Why give your life and work to a group and then not invest the few hours it takes to work things through with a person? People often keep quiet out of consideration for someone until they get so angry they want to throw the person out altogether.

At one time or another you, too, may have felt discouraged about the group, unwilling to do the work, anxious you weren't doing it right. Help hear the person who is having these feelings today, even if today you don't feel that way.

It helps, in a group, to invite a person to speak who has just made motions or grunts and didn't get a chance to express anything.

If a person says something meaningful and then a lot of trivial things are said by others or irrelevant questions are asked, return to the first person with an invitation to say more.

When all are down on one person, there has to be someone who is more interested in letting that person get heard than in joining the attack. Even if you feel insecure or an outsider in the group, you can always express your wish to hear more from any person, or to have that person repeat something to which the group didn't respond.

There are ways to help with an interaction between two other people. If two or more are having trouble, and you are not too upset yourself, you can help each person get heard. In a bad interaction, usually neither person can hear the other very well. If you respond to one person, as in the first stage of listening, the other can hear you and see the good results of the process. Then turn and respond to the second person's feelings. That lets the first one listen. (Don't mediate and decide who's right about what. Keep your view for later, or maybe say it fast and get back to them.)

Most of what we've said about listening can help in interactions with the people close to you. The difference is that you aren't trying *only* to help; you're also trying to live and work; so expect it to be harder and slower. Accept it if you can't do as well when you personally are involved. Don't be surprised if you can't listen well when you're being attacked. Even just trying these approaches—no matter how slow or hard it seems— sometimes gets people out of a stuck atmosphere.

A big difference can be made in a group if you listen, if you focus and say some of what you find, and if you ask others sometimes to sense and say more of what they are feeling.

PART FOUR

Focusing
and Society

Chapter 12
New Relationships

People find richness in each other as they open up in focusing and listening.

As a result, relationships grow fuller and more solid. An appreciative climate develops. In each person a striving for rightness is sensed and respected.

Focusing can help free stuck relationships—even those that have been stuck for a long time. Consider, for instance, the case of Ken and Ed, two professors at my university. They had an argument almost twenty years ago. It didn't get resolved. Ever since, they have avoided each other except at official meetings. They are often both involved in decisions that matter to them. They cannot avoid talking to each other. Their relationship is not bitter, only stuck. They don't do anything deliberately to trouble each other, but nothing helpful either.

A few years ago I was involved in one of their decisions. I sat in Ken's office as he pondered the decision. He knew what he wanted, but he also guessed that Ed would have complicated feelings about it, probably in opposition. Ken needed Ed's support. At least he needed Ed not to oppose actively. Ken decided to approach Ed directly. But how did he do it? Ken decided to approach Ed *on the phone* to talk about it, even though Ed was in the same building. Nothing much changed, of course.

These two do not know about focusing and listening.

They think they know each other, and of course, in a sense they do. They have observed each other for twenty years. Each predicts correctly what the other will do in a given situation. But they don't know that a shift could happen if they focused and listened to each other. They don't sense the richness that lies just beneath the disagreeable traits each knows in the other. *They don't know there can be movement in such stuck places.*

The usual thing to say to them would *not* be useful. "Why don't the two of you just talk it over?" That would only result in more bad feelings. Each would probably begin by saying what's wrong with the other. If they did, they would only justify their opinions of each other and also justify their general view that people are what they are and stay that way.

But in a real focusing-listening process both could change. The change needed in each one isn't drastic: only a change in how each feels about the other.

Ken, underneath those traits and habits that bother Ed, is different from what either man suspects without focusing. If that rich human texture could emerge, both would feel different.

In arguments both people endlessly repeat their positions, over and over. It saves a lot of time if you restate the other's position: "I don't agree but let me see if I know what you're saying. Your point is..." This permits the other person to stop repeating, and to listen to you, or to focus and see what else he feels.

Or let's take an example from a closer relationship. She wants the freedom to have more than one lover. He is jealous and anxious. They have been stuck there for some time.

Their interaction has repeatedly gone something like

this: whenever she felt comfortable with him, she would express her love for him but also mention her need to go out with others. He would question her. Go out with whom? When? How often? She would lock herself into silence and resentfulness. Then they would be stuck.

His "knowing" her went this far: he sensed that she then felt withdrawn, but he didn't understand why.

Her "knowing" him was in terms of his possessiveness. She saw him as wanting to own her, limit her life.

At last, after months of this, they focused and listened. One step went this way: he said, "When I ask you those questions and you get mad and won't talk to me, what are your feelings? I can listen now, for a change."

Instead of repeating her usual complaint about his possessiveness, she focused. For a while she stayed silent, and so did he. Then she got it: "What makes me so angry, Hank, is that when you ask those things you suddenly turn into an unattractive, unromantic, scared man for me, and I lose my sexual turn-on for you. That's really what happens."

He simply said, "Oh, I didn't know that. I'm glad you found that and told me."

This one focusing step did not solve their whole problem, of course. But even this one step had the effect of moving their relationship on past a stuck point.

Focusing can save time. It might take only a few minutes a day. You get to where the trouble is and it shifts. How much more efficient that is than to be stuck in an unchanging relationship, spending time and energy on repetitious quarrels that go nowhere.

It seems obvious that close relationships can benefit from regular focusing and listening. But how about work situations? Wouldn't everyone become too close personally? Might the atmosphere grow too sticky? Would people talk deeply with each other all the time so no work could get done? Imagine spending fifteen minutes listening to someone every time you go to the purchasing department for a simple form!

No, it wouldn't be like that. Rather, it's more like that *without* focusing and listening!

Most workplaces are dense with bad feeling and bad relationships. Every time Rhena goes to the purchasing department, she has to take those sick smiles from that woman who last year tried to get her fired. Bill is destructive and doesn't trust anybody, and Jim plays along with him and tells him every bad thing about all the others. And so on.

Many people work every day in places like that. And even in pleasant places, work would be expedited if people would listen.

People like to get work done, and done well. They get discouraged because in most places there are too many ways to get stuck.

It will take much time to improve our work situations, our schools, hospitals, churches. Spaces and times for focusing and listening can be made in any institution. But even when focusing and listening are learned by everyone (probably in schools), our workplaces and institutions will still change slowly.

Our structured institutions today offer little opportunity for personal living and speaking. The real living of people is mostly dulled and silent, inside them, alone. In terms of social institutions, *that* space is empty.

If you want to meet someone more personally, modern society offers only a few poor choices. You can go to psychotherapy. You can attend a weekend encounter group. If it is successful (about one out of three is), you will come close to some people and they will come close to you. Then it breaks up. If you want more, then a week later a new group of strangers confronts you. You can have the same initial experience over again, but there is no continuing social structure.

What is the answer? I believe it lies in a new kind of social structure called a "Changes" group.[1]

Several such groups have been developed over the years, in various parts of the country, by people who know focusing and listening. Such a group brings people together in the closeness of focusing–listening. What is important is that it is *there*—a continuing social structure. It is a place where you can go when you need to focus and need someone to listen to you.

You can very easily start a Changes group yourself. To show you how such groups work, let me describe one of them: Changes in Chicago.

On a typical Sunday evening, there is a big meeting in the church at 57th and University Avenue. Two large rooms are full of people. You look more closely and see that they are in pairs. At many little tables, in corners, and in the hall you see two people sitting. One talks, one listens. After some time they will reverse roles.

If you had walked in earlier you would have seen a large meeting of the whole group. You would have seen listening in action. Someone says something important.

---

1. Changes was started by Kristin Glaser.

Someone else turns to the speaker and says, "I think what you're getting at is . . ." The speaker pauses, focuses briefly and says, "Well, yes, but more like . . ."

I am always impressed at Changes when this happens so regularly. Although I have trained people in listening for many, many years, I often forget to listen when I am in a big group. I am always glad when others don't forget. If I interrupt, someone says, "Wait, Gene, I think she's trying to say . . ."

Once in a while, someone shy will want to say something difficult and will ask an individual in the group to listen. It looks odd. I remember Susan standing up at a meeting and saying, "Um . . . Joe, will you listen to me so I can get this out?" Joe nods. She says something and Joe says back the crux of it. She continues and so does Joe. In this way she gets her thoughts said and heard, before anyone else in the group can interrupt or argue. Everyone understands what she wanted Joe to do and why.

Another purpose of listening in that community would become clear to you during the break. People mill around and talk in little informal groups, as they do anywhere else. Someone comes up to a man and says, "Hello, Tom. I'm going through a tough time and I need to be listened to. Are you in a shape to do it?" "Sure," Tom says. "Does it need to be right now?" "Well, yes, if that's OK." They walk off to find some quiet corner.

Or Tom might have said, "No, I don't want to listen now. Sorry." The focuser would walk off to find another listener. Or Tom might have suggested a time for some other day. Or he might have said, "Yes, sure, but I need a listener, too. Can we share the time?"

As we've noted before in this book, real listening is

rare. When Allan moved to a job in Tucson, he would come back to Chicago every few months, just *to be listened to!*

Once people experience what is at first vague and murky opening into step after step of one's inner detail and change, then living without this in people becomes lonely and shallow. Without some people who listen, it is hard to hear oneself. One is often frustrated with people who don't know focusing. Every little while one wants to say, "Could you go see more what that is?" but the person doesn't know what that means.

People think they already know what they feel. They may be in excellent touch with their "gut feelings," but then they let it go at that. They don't know that a road of many steps would open if they sensed beyond the obvious feelings, into what is not as yet clear.

So one usually wants to teach focusing to those with whom one wants to be close. Not that one must hear what comes. In silence, too, it is good.

It is lonely also if I am taken as static in what I feel and say, if you won't listen knowing that there can be steps into depth, and shifts. It is boring if you take what I express as my "position," and in response you state yours. Then we are done. We are both flat, like a closed door in a wall.

It is not surprising that Allan came to Chicago to be listened to. Now that these skills are spreading, Changes is no longer such a rare island.

After the mutual listening part of the Changes evening, there is a short break. Then people go to special groups. There are listening–training groups. There are several focusing groups in which a very gentle climate prevails, and they would be shy to let you in. There are also other activities. Someone might have stood up spontaneously in the big group and said, "I would like to lead a dance movement group tonight. Meet me in this corner." Or it might have been behavior modification or a group on Jungian dream interpretation.

Focusing makes all other methods more effective by putting them in relation to the body's felt sense. We don't make a "sect" of focusing. It goes well with, and can be added to, anything a person already finds helpful. Conversely, we are glad for anyone to teach us other skills. People talk about different methods as though they contradict each other, but in the human body what helps doesn't contradict anything else that helps. Focusing lets you sense whether something is helpful for you at a given time.

Self-help skill training is essential for such a network, and focusing and listening involve specific steps in which anyone can be trained.

You would often find more real psychotherapy happening in that community than in formal therapy. It might worry you to see seemingly untrained people doing this. What if Tom is no good at listening, or what if he pushes his views on others? Is this safe?

It is safer than doctors. No one thinks the other person is an authority. No one here is likely to put up with being told what to do, imposed upon, or interrupted. The person they have asked to listen is just another person. If Tom's listening doesn't feel good, the focuser will go away.

A psychotherapy patient who is getting little from therapy requires months or years to change therapists. Usually, the patient thinks, "The doctor *must* know what's going on. There *must* be good reasons for it." Changes is far safer than psychotherapy. When psychotherapy is effective, it is irreplaceable, but then the patient can feel some changes going on in the body.

How can you start your own Changes group? Begin by finding one person who will focus and listen with you. If that works out and you both want a Changes group, invite a third person in, and plan gradually to let others in. Encourage each person who likes it to bring others.

What makes any Changes group work is the focusing–listening approach. There is no need for a "policy," and Changes as a whole has none. Of course, there are housekeeping decisions. Someone has to decide when to meet, what to do with small amounts of money, and so on.

In the traditional organizational model—not at Changes—such decisions are handled by a small power group others cannot join. Another model is "participatory democracy," in which everyone tries to make all decisions. But decisions are boring, people grow impatient, and meetings get rancorous, even though the decision being made is trivial.

Changes has a third model. There is a small group that makes housekeeping decisions. But everyone knows where and when it meets and is always invited to be part of it: for one time, occasionally, steadily, or never. Most members don't come, but all may.

Each Changes group is organized as its own members want it. There is a "Changes International," but it only keeps a list of Changes groups and mails out occasional literature. It enforces no "policy."

Focusing and listening are not the only things practiced, or the only viewpoint. But they are shared and learned by all who wish to. There is much therapeutic changing and human closeness.

Chapter 13
Experience Beyond Roles

In our time an advance in the nature of the human individual is occurring.

Throughout history people expressed themselves in routine patterns of language, and understood themselves that way, too. Types of emotional experiences were labeled: if someone cheated you, you were angry; if someone gave you something, grateful. No doubt people suspected that there was more to it all than that—more than one could say or understand—but nobody knew quite what that "more" was.

To express ourselves (even to ourselves) and to handle our situations, we need to get into this "more" of our own experience. At first this "more" revealed certain causes and contents that seemed to be the same for every person. Of course, there was no agreement on just what these universal contents were, and several systems arose to say what they are. Then, more deeply, it was discovered that beyond systems the unique individual emerges.

In the most recent years there has been a great development: millions of people have "gotten in touch with their feelings." If one has not been accustomed to turn inward to one's feelings very often, it is a big life-step to do so. Many methods and movements exist that have this as their essence.

Focusing is a different, further step. Beyond contacting feelings there is a different inward "place." *A holistic body sense, at first unclear*, can form. It is a sense of the whole meaning of a particular concern. *It is from this "place"* that a series of inward shifts, a road of many steps, can arise. An inward texture of detail reveals itself and changes.

We found focusing by studying patients who already did it. We didn't invent it. We only made it specific and teachable.

Human experience, we now understand, does not really consist of pieces or contents that have a static shape. As one senses the exact, finely complex shape at a given moment, it also changes in this very sensing.

A person's experience cannot be *figured out* by others, or even by the person experiencing it. It cannot be expressed in common labels. It has to be met, found, felt, attended to, and allowed to show itself.

A vignette will help show what I mean.

I had been asked to teach listening and focusing to a group of psychotherapists and student therapists. One woman, a therapist-in-training, didn't feel like an equal in this group. It contained only one other woman. It included her supervisor, several co-workers, a man who was her therapist, and me, the visiting teacher.

When it was her turn to say a little about a problem (so we could practice listening), she said her husband insisted that she talk when she came home. He had aided her long struggle for professional training, and now he wanted her to share her experiences with him. It was only fair. Yet when she came home she wanted to rest, to be in herself. She wanted to be able to refuse.

I obeyed the rules of good listening and said just that:

"You long to be in yourself, to rest, to be able to refuse. Is that right?"

Something inside her suddenly seemed to uncramp. She looked up and her eyes glistened. "Yes, to be able to refuse! To be able to go by my own needing and feeling! To let that count for something even in relation to another person! Yes, yes!"

The others had some questions. Was she not being selfish, hostile? Was she not avoiding contact with another human? Wasn't she showing some lack of mature development by her need to withdraw in order to find herself? Whole chains of deductions could be made from the little she had said, and many routine labels could be applied to it.

No one seemed to want to take what she had said as she had said it. Everyone seemed to want *something else*, something she *didn't* say, to be what was "really" there. I had "only" listened.

She braved the supervisor, the therapist, and the others. Now she could feel that she knew exactly what she was experiencing. It resonated in her. The words touched the experience, and the experience supported the words.

She had discovered, through being heard accurately, that her feeling had its own personal shape and being.

But couldn't one argue that this woman's experience fits a common pattern? The woman who asserts the reality of her own experience: isn't this pattern 17B, so to speak?

No, a person's experience is not a pattern. It might seem to fit a pattern just now, but moments later it will fit another or none. In any case, the seeming fit will never be exact, for experience is richer than patterns. Moreover, it is changing.

Experience is unique when focusing has unfolded it. As someone told me once, in regard to a room in which we did a lot of focusing and listening: "In there, what goes on has never happened before in the history of the world." He meant that each person's unique experience, as it went through steps of focusing, had never been encountered before. But he also meant to point to the fact that in history, until now, ordinary people have not generally done this.

It is a new step in human development when people can not only get in touch with their feelings but then also move through steps of unfolding and change. We are moving beyond conformity patterns.

Nonconformity has always been possible, of course. But those who rejected traditional patterns often found themselves adrift, lost, without values and standards. Focusing replaces those patterns with a way of making new patterns.

If we are busily discarding old forms and patterns, what will replace them? New forms that are equally fixed and painful? New forms can come from *inside* each person instead of being imposed from outside. A world in which this happens won't be a world in which people get forced into forms that cramp and hurt. It will be a world in which *forms are used in a new way*.

Let's examine this possibility in a little more detail.

Many people today are struggling with a baffling fact: The old patterns that are supposed to make life work—and once did—no longer serve. Being a parent today, for example, doesn't work if we try to do it as our parents did, yet no other form is established for us to follow. We have to make it up as we go along—often learning that what we just did was wrong.

Similarly, some women find the housewife role empty and intolerable, but are often unprepared for anything else even if they know what it might be. The pattern of being a woman is changing, but people argue whether it is changing into this or that new pattern, as if eventually, somehow, a fixed form must be imposed.

And what are the proper roles for sons and daughters? Can you become your own person yet still care for your parents? This is a question each young person confronts.

These old patterns once were useful. The mass of people (always with odd exceptions) fitted themselves into the roles and routines they were assigned and which gave them an inner life of emotions. Only a small number of educated and thinking people *created* roles and patterns.

But today this dependence on routines and roles has changed. A large part of the *mass* of people are educated and literate. The creativity and creative needs of people have expanded, and now the routines are too confining. People find that they have feelings that are far more complex than accepted roles either demand or offer.

How can more developed individuals make a better social structure? It is a large, unsolved problem. We know a lot about how social patterns form individuals, but if one begins with individuals . . . there is a gap. We don't know how individual development can ever reach the level of social structure. That is why there has been so little progress in the character of social and political units.

Focusing is only a piece of an answer. It lets people find

their own inner source of direction. It can be a source of new patterns, devised freshly by each individual.

Instead of static structures we need structure-making. This would not be unstructured. Without structure nothing happens. It would be an expected and understood constant restructuring. Social situations could be structured so that they could be restructured by the participants.

Instead of having only the predictable, expected emotions the roles call for, we often have unclear feelings. They are unclear because "clear" feelings are those that are already patterned. We must make new phrases to express these unclear feelings, and new forms of action to carry the feelings into daily life. This is the process of form-making.

To an extent, we are all engaged increasingly in *the form-making process*.

This is where the big change can come from. If we accept ourselves and each other as form-makers, we will no longer need to force forms on ourselves or each other.

Today most people still assume that a new set of forms will eventually be agreed upon. The implication is that, as before, we will have to force those new forms on ourselves and each other.

It is true that a lot of this old-style form-forcing is still going on. For example, people now think the new role pattern is not to be jealous or possessive. If their spouse or lover is having a sexual relationship with someone else, they feel they should accept it. But they don't. Then they go through vast struggles with themselves to force the new role pattern on themselves. Free sex is the new form; and while they are ready to change the old, the new one forced on them may not fit either. Endless hurt goes on, along with feelings of guilt and self-blame, because the new form doesn't fit. "What's wrong with me?" the question goes. "If this form fits everybody else who is brave and new, why doesn't it fit me?" Only the form is new. This is the usual way of conforming to forms, old and new.

Some couples who know focusing are developing unique and differentiated ways of opening their relationships. Others say they have a new respect for jealousy as they can feel it in their bodies. What *is* clear is that adopting general patterns, old or new, is not the way. Our bodies constantly absorb new learnings, additions to their already gigantic store of wisdom. Real learning can occur only in dialogue with one's body. A sensitive focusing approach can eventuate in really livable patterns suited uniquely to each of us and our close people. Let us adopt the pattern-*making*.

The feelings seem like inner things, strong and often unchanging. To reveal that a feeling is not a thing, one must sense beyond it. It is different to sense the whole of a situation as a not yet clear body-sense.

Feelings often conflict with reason. Many feelings are *less* wise than reason, yet reason alone is rarely enough to change us, or to rely on.

The holistic felt sense is more inclusive than reason. It *includes* the reasons of reason as well as what made the feeling, and much more. That holistic sense can be lived further, and has its own directionality. It is your sense of the whole thing, including what you know, have thought, have learned. It includes both what you think you "ought" and what is not yet resolved. Thought and feeling, ought and want, are not now split in it.

Said one person: "More and more I want that inner sense of knowing that I get now sometimes. I wish I had it all the time."

What is at first sensed unclearly and holistically is more basic than the thoughts, feelings, and ways of acting that are already formed, already cut out into existing patterns.

A society of pattern-makers is coming. It cannot help but be a society in which people are also more sensitive to, and intolerant of, social brutalities and oppressions, and more able to act to change them.

Appendix

A.

Philosophical Note

Focusing is part of a wider philosophy (see Philosophical References). In focusing one pays attention to a "felt sense." This is felt in the body, yet it has meanings. It has all the meanings one is already living with because one lives in situations with one's body. A felt sense is body *and* mind before they are split apart.

What is the relation between this unsplit body-mind and our more usual logical thinking? I have dealt with this question systematically in my philosophical works.

Focusing is not an invitation to drop thinking and just feel. That would leave our feelings unchanged. Focusing begins with that odd and little known "felt sense," and then we think verbally, logically, or with image forms— but in such a way that the felt sense shifts. When there is a body shift, we sense that our usual kind of thinking has come together with body-mind, and has succeeded in letting body-mind move a step.

What we can trust is not just body-mind, not just thought, not even such a step. We trust the series of steps.

Thinking in the usual way can be objectively true and powerful. But, when put in touch with what the body already knows and lives, it becomes vastly more powerful.

There is a new method here, not only for personal concerns but also for theory and science. Logical thinking stays within whatever "conceptual boxes" it starts with. It has only the different, competing interpretations, assumptions, viewpoints—and one must stay within one of these. When felt sense is the touchstone, one can try out all kinds of different concepts without being locked into any one set. This is what scientists (now rarely) do when they come up with something new after living with a problem for a long time. Rather than using concepts only, one can return to one's unsplit felt sense of whatever one is working on.

One can keep whatever each set of concepts or assumptions shows, and yet also go free of them and go directly to the felt sense. In that way one can emerge with something else that those concepts could never arrive at, and make new concepts.

A new basic model, a new way of understanding experience and nature, is involved. Experience and nature are not like our concepts. Truth does not lie in thought alone. It lies in how various thoughts relate to experience, whether they bring something into focus from experience or not.

Experience can never be equated with concepts. But experience is not "undefined" either. It is *more* organized, more finely faceted by far, than any concepts can be. And yet it is always again able to be lived further in a new creation of meaning that takes account of, and also shifts, all the earlier meanings.

How this relation between concepts and experience changes logic and conceptual structure has been presented elsewhere.

This philosophy leads to a new method of human thinking.

In my philosophical works I have found ways to deal

with the well-known problems surrounding the word "experience," the activity of language beyond what can be represented and other problems that currently seem to make the above impossible.

See Philosophical References.

B.
Research, Applications, and References

(Many of these are available at www.focusing.org)

There have been over 100 research studies showing the effectiveness of the Focusing and High Experiencing Scale Level in various applications (Hendricks, 2001, available at www.focusing.org).

Focusing is being studied in relation to concerns as far apart as spirituality, business, problem solving, creative writing, medicine, children, sports, and theory construction.

Focusing applies to more than personal problems. Creativity, originality, and depth require something like focusing in any field: the capacity to attend to what is not yet verbalized. This might be about something intellectual, practical, or anything else.

Philosophical References

Gendlin, E. T. (1997). *Experiencing and the Creation of Meaning. A Philosophical and Psychological Approach to the Subjective.* Paperback. Northwestern University Press (1997), with a new Preface.

Gendlin, E. T. (1997). *A Process Model.* The Focusing Institute: www.focusing.org.

Gendlin, E. T. (1997). "The Responsive Order: A New Empiricism." *Man and World*, 30 (3), 383–411.

Gendlin, E. T. (1995). Crossing and Dipping: Some Terms for Approaching the Interface Between Natural Understanding and Logical Formation. *Minds and Machines*, 5(4), 547–560.

Gendlin, E. T. (1992). "The Primacy of the Body, Not the Primacy of Perception." *Man and World*, 25 (3–4), 341–353.

Gendlin, E. T. (1991). "Thinking Beyond Patterns: Body, Language and Situations." In: den Ouden, B., and Moen, M. (Eds.), *The Presence of Feeling in Thought*, pp. 25–151. Frankfurt-New York: Peter Lang.

Levin, D. M. (Ed.) (1997). *Language Beyond Postmodernism: Saying and Thinking in Gendlin's Philosophy*. Evanston: Northwestern University Press.

References

Campbell, P. and McMahon, E. (1985). *Bio-Spirituality: Focusing As a Way to Grow*. Chicago, IL: Loyola University Press.

Elbow, P. and Belanoff, P. (1989). "Private Writing: Finding What You Have to Say." *A Community of Writers: A Workshop Course in Writing*.

Flanagan, K. (1998). *Everyday Genius: Focusing on Your Emotional Intelligence*. Dublin, Ireland: Marino.

Focusing and Medicine (1999). The Folio: A Journal for Focusing and Experiential Therapy. The Focusing Institute.

Focusing with Children (1997). The Folio: A Journal for Focusing and Experiential Therapy. The Focusing Institute.

Friedman, N. (1995). *On Focusing: How to Access Your Own and Other People's Direct Experience*. Arlington, MA.

Friedman, N. (2000). *Focusing: Selected Essays* 1974–1999. Xlibris Corp.

Gendlin, E. T. (1986). *Let Your Body Interpret Your Dreams*. Wilmette, IL: Chiron.

Gendlin, E .T. (1996). *Focusing-Oriented Psychotherapy. A Manual of the Experiential Method*. New York: Guilford.

Hendricks, M.N. (2001). Focusing-Oriented/Experiential Psychotherapy: Research and Practice." In: Cain, D. and Seeman, J. (Eds.), *Handbook of Research and Practice in Humanistic Psychotherapies*, American Psychological Association: Washington D.C.

Hendricks, M. N. (1986). "Experiencing Level as a Therapeutic Variable," *Person-Centered Review,* Vol. I, No. 2, May 1986, 141–162. Sage Publications Inc.

Hinterkopf, Elfie (1998). *Integrating Spirituality in Counseling: A Manual for Using the Experiential Focusing Method*. Virginia: American Counseling Association.

Ikemi, A. (2000). *Presence, Existence & Space: Key Concepts in Focusing-Oriented Psychotherapy*, Nada Lou Productions, Canada (VHS video). See also http://www.ne.jp/asahi/focusing/jfa/j-focusing-e.html

Klagsbrun, J. (1999). *How I Teach a Focusing Workshop*. The Focusing Institute.

Klagsbrun, J. (2001). "Listening and Focusing: Holistic Health Care Tools for Nurses." In: *Holistic Nursing Care*, Vol. 36, No. 1, pp. 115–129

Klein, J. (1998). *Inside-Me Stories: "Something Is Happening Inside-Me!"* The Inside People Press.

Sherman, E. (1990). "Experiential Reminiscence and Life-Review Therapy with the Elderly." In: Lietaer, G., Rombauts,

J., and Van Balen, R. (Eds.), *Client-Centered and Experiential Psychotherapy in the Nineties* (pp. 709–732). Leuven, Belgium: Leuven University Press.

Weiser Cornell, Ann. (1996). *The Power of Focusing.* Oakland, CA: New Harbinger Publications.

Wiltschko, J. (1994). "Focusing Therapy: Some Fragments in Which the Whole Can Become Visible." In: Hutterer, R., Pawlowsky, G., Schmid, P.F., and Stipsits, R. (Eds.), *Client-Centered and Experiential Psychotherapy.* Frankfurt/New York: Peter Lang, 1996.

Wolfus, B. and Bierman, R. (1996). "An Evaluation of a Group Treatment Program for Incarcerated Male Batterers." *International Journal of Offender Therapy and Comparative Criminology,* 40, 318–333.

C.
Directory

You must judge any human process by your own direct bodily experience. Even if you choose one of our best focusing teachers—if what happens does not feel good, "like fresh air," then it isn't focusing that is happening. Or, if it is supposed to be therapy, then it isn't really therapy that is happening. This principle applies not just to this directory but to any supposedly helpful process for your life and person.

WE NOW HAVE FOCUSING TEACHERS IN 125 CITIES IN THE U.S. ALONE, AND IN 31 OTHER COUNTRIES.

FOR A FOCUSING TEACHER NEAR YOU (OR WORKSHOPS, OR THE LATEST DEVELOPMENTS IN FOCUSING) PLEASE CONSULT OUR WEB SITE AT WWW.FOCUSING.ORG.

EUGENE T. GENDLIN, PH.D.
THE FOCUSING INSTITUTE
34 EAST LANE
SPRING VALLEY, NY 10977
TEL./FAX: (845) 362-5222
INFO@FOCUSING.ORG
WWW.FOCUSING.ORG

At www.focusing.org

- Find a focusing partner (you take turns and divide the time)
- Find a focusing workshop near you
- Find a focusing teacher or therapist near you
- Visit our online bookstore (audio- and videotapes also)
- Visit the Children's Corner
- Be on our mailing list
- Become a member to get our newsletter, journal, and workshop announcements
- Find articles on focusing in psychotherapy, medicine, creative writing, with children and in other areas

The Focusing Institute is a not-for-profit organization founded in 1986. Its mission is to make focusing available to the academic and scholarly communities and to the public at large. We are an international community of people who focus.

Focusing Partnerships

Many people all over the world have a focusing partnership. They receive a half hour of attention from another person and then give that person a half hour of their attention at least once a week at a regular time, usually on the phone.

Most people focus on their main concerns of that day, which might be the next thing to do in their work, inner experiences, their attempts to develop as people, a difficult letter to write—or whatever they find uppermost.

Your partner offers no advice, no judgments, no comments. We have learned that people can go deeper and arrive at creative steps forward if the listener refrains from adding anything. Judgments, advice, and comments express the person who is giving them, not the person he or she is listening to. Your partner will tell you honestly whether he or she is following you or not. For example, "My mind wandered. Would you please repeat that for me."

As focusers we only say as much about something as we want to say. We can enter deeply into ourselves in our own privacy.

D.

Focusing: Short Form

1. Clear a space

How are you? What's between you and feeling fine?
Don't answer; let what comes in your body do the answering.
Don't go into anything.
Greet each concern that comes. Put each aside for a while, next to you.
Except for that, are you fine?

2. Felt sense

Pick one problem to focus on.
Don't go into the problem. What do you sense in your body when you recall the whole of that problem?
Sense all of that, the sense of the whole thing, the murky discomfort or the unclear body-sense of it.

3. Get a handle

What is the quality of the felt sense?
What one word, phrase, or image comes out of this felt sense?
What quality-word would fit it best?

4. Resonate

Go back and forth between word (or image) and the felt sense. Is that right?
If they match, have the sensation of matching several times.

If the felt sense changes, follow it with your attention.

When you get a perfect match, the words (images) being just right for this feeling, let yourself feel that for a minute.

5. Ask

"What is it, about the whole problem, that makes me so——?"

When stuck, ask questions:
What is the worst of this feeling?
What's really so bad about this?
What does it need?
What should happen?
Don't answer; wait for the feeling to stir and give you an answer.

What would it feel like if it was all OK?
Let the body answer:
What is in the way of that?

6. Receive

Welcome what came. Be glad it spoke.
It is only one step on this problem, not the last.
Now that you know where it is, you can leave it and come back to it later.
Protect it from critical voices that interrupt.

Does your body want another round of focusing, or is this a good stopping place?

About the Author

Eugene T. Gendlin received his Ph.D. in philosophy from the University of Chicago and taught there from 1963 to 1995. He has been honored three times by the American Psychological Association for his development of experiential psychotherapy. He received the first Distinguished Professional Psychologist of the Year award from the Clinical Division and an award from the Philosophical Psychology Division; he and the Focusing Institute received an award from the Humanistic Division in 2000. He was the founder and editor for many years of the Clinical Division journal *Psychotherapy: Theory, Research and Practice*. His book *Focusing* has sold over 500,000 copies and is translated into seventeen languages. His other books include *Let Your Body Interpret Your Dreams, Focusing-Oriented Psychotherapy, Experiencing and the Creation of Meaning, Language Beyond Post-Modernism: Saying and Thinking in Gendlin's Philosophy* (edited by David Levin), and *A Process Model*. He has published many articles and is internationally recognized as a major American philosopher and psychologist. A complete bibliography and the full text of more than a hundred articles are available at www.focusing.org/gendlin/.